The God of
the Poor

The God of
the Poor

Gerald Kaufman

Destiny Image Publishers
P.O. Box 310
Shippensburg, PA 17257

"Tapping the Power of the Age to Come"

ISBN 1-56043-778-2

For Worldwide Distribution
Printed in the U.S.A.

Destiny Image books are available through these fine distributors outside the United States:

Christian Growth, Inc. Jalan Kilang-Timor, Singapore 0315	Successful Christian Living Capetown, Rep. of South Africa
Lifestream Nottingham, England	Vision Resources Ponsonby, Auckland, New Zealand
Rhema Ministries Trading Randburg, South Africa	WA Buchanan Company Geebung, Queensland, Australia
Salvation Book Centre Petaling, Jaya, Malaysia	Word Alive Niverville, Manitoba, Canada

Contents

Introduction

The Spirit of the Lord is upon Me, because He hath anointed Me to preach the gospel to the poor; He hath sent Me to heal the brokenhearted, to preach deliverance to the captives, and recovering of sight to the blind, to set at liberty them that are bruised, to preach the acceptable year of the Lord.

Luke 4:18-19

Preaching the gospel to the poor is the central vision of the church I pastor (Love Gospel Assembly, Bronx, NY), and it is the very thing God desires to bring forth in the Body of Christ. Webster's Dictionary defines *the poor* as "those who lack material possessions and have little or no means to support themselves." The poor are the needy, impoverished and destitute. Interestingly, the Word of God is filled from cover to cover with references to the positive responses required of God's people toward the poor.

As I studied week by week in preparation for a series of sermons imparting a vision for ministry to the poor, my life was changed. I hope this book will change your life as well. Whatever the conclusions you may come to, the fact remains that this message is the heart of God. When we give serious attention to those for whom Jesus cares, though no one else seems concerned, we are obeying the will of God, and it will change our lives.

Many things being preached on television today are not edifying, especially the teaching which implies that God lives to make us rich. This philosophy, which seems to prevail through this country, appears to be the gospel, but it is not. Congruently, there are ministers standing on pulpits condemning the poor simply because they are poor. It is not always the poor people's fault! Oftentimes poverty is the fault of other people through suppression, oppression, afflictions and injustices; yet, we mock the poor. What we really are doing is reproaching God. "He who mocks the poor reproaches his Maker..." (Prov. 17:5, NAS).

We have tended to assume that the sin of Sodom was singular, but I am going to show you that it was twofold. We have emphasized the sexual aspect of Sodom's sin in order to circumvent another aspect. In so doing we have not properly interpreted Scripture. Let us explore the other aspect of Sodom's sinfulness.

> *Behold, this was the iniquity of thy sister Sodom, pride, fulness of bread, and abundance of idleness was in her and in her daughters, neither did she strengthen the hand of the poor and needy. And they were haughty, and committed abomination before Me: therefore I took them away as I saw good.*

> Ezekiel 16:49-50

While there was abundance of bread and pride because of their affluence, Sodom neglected the poor. The Sodomites had much wealth, but because of their idleness they were unable to accomplish anything. They were not only caught up in abominations of all sorts, but they also neglected the poor. Consequently, neglect of the poor was one of the main reasons God destroyed Sodom. God denounced their neglect of the poor before He even mentioned their other abominations. Cities and countries cannot stand when they neglect the poor.

The teaching of the poor and about the poor, however, is not to be exclusive. Many believe that we should either be rich and preach wealth or be poor and preach poverty. There is no virtue in riches, nor is there any inherent holiness in poverty. The Church of Jesus Christ is not a Church exclusively for poor people, nor is it exclusively for the rich. We cannot go from one type of exclusivity to another. What I preach is a concern of the Body of Christ for the poor.

In teaching a seminar on the inner city, I was really speaking for the poor and taking a stand for them. A brother stood up and asked, "Brother Kaufman, if those people that are poor have accepted Jesus, why are they still poor?" I replied, "Because people like you who have accepted Jesus are still rich." Evidently, that brother had no intention to ever share a dollar with a poor person, but rather to put him down. If God has blessed us financially, it is to help us be a vehicle through which He blesses the poor and builds His Kingdom. The point is that today, as in other times, the poor are neglected.

It is the purpose of this book to set forth the need to preach the gospel of Jesus Christ to the poor. This vision is too big for one local church; we all must meet the needs of the poor. This is not a cliché, but a commitment that we as a church have made. We challenge you to participate with us. I pray that as you read the following chapters, God will add revelation to your understanding of what He is saying. *God is not the God of poverty, but He is the God of the poor.*

Chapter One

The Message for the Poor

...He hath anointed Me to preach the gospel to the poor....

Luke 4:18

Today the preaching of the gospel essentially is directed to the rich and middle class, rather than to the poor. Neither the poor nor the rich are more spiritual than the other, but the poor are more neglected. However, the poor are more receptive to the gospel because of their greater physical needs.

It is messianic to preach the gospel to the poor. Before getting into the main text, let us look at a portion of Scripture found in the Gospel of Matthew:

And it came to pass, when Jesus had made an end of commanding His twelve disciples, He departed thence to teach and to preach in their cities. Now when John had heard in the prison the works of Christ, he sent two of his disciples, and said unto Him, Art Thou He that should come, or do we look for another? Jesus answered and said unto them, Go and show John again those things which ye do hear and see: The blind receive their sight, and the lame walk, the lepers are cleansed, and the deaf hear, the dead are raised up, and the poor have the gospel preached to them.

Matthew 11:1-5

Verse 5 gives proof that Jesus is the Messiah. When He made the statement, "...and the poor have the gospel preached to them," Jesus obviously was inferring that no one was preaching the gospel to the poor. He was saying that all the religious people (the Sadducees and the Pharisees) could not see the poor, rather they only saw themselves and their own needs.

And He came to Nazareth, where He had been brought up: and, as His custom was, He went into the synagogue on the sabbath day, and stood up for to read. And there was delivered unto Him the book of the prophet [Isaiah]. And when He had opened the book, He found the place where it was written, The Spirit of the Lord is upon Me, because He hath anointed Me to preach the gospel to the poor; He hath sent Me to heal the brokenhearted, to preach deliverance to the captives, and recovering of sight to the blind, to set at liberty them that are bruised, to preach the acceptable year of the Lord. And He closed the book, and He gave it again to the minister, and sat down. And the eyes of all them that were in the synagogue were fastened on Him. And He began to say unto them, This day is this scripture fulfilled in your ears.

Luke 4:16-21

The Scripture quoted in Luke 4 is a messianic passage from Isaiah 61. In the synagogue, Jesus was claiming that He was the Messiah. He was stating His credentials as the Messiah. He came to preach the gospel to the poor, to heal the brokenhearted, preach deliverance to the captives, give recovery of sight to the blind and set at liberty those who are bruised. The word *bruised* used in this setting means "oppressed."

By paying close attention to the text, one can see that God is the God of the poor. This is not to say that God is the God of poverty, rather He is the God of the poor.

In this book we will examine

1. *The message for the poor*, "...to preach the gospel to the poor...."
2. *The medicine for the poor*, "...to heal the broken-hearted...."
3. *The miracle for the poor*, "...to preach deliverance to the captives...."
4. *The manifestation for the poor*, "...recovering of sight to the blind...."
5. *The mercy for the poor*, "...to set at liberty them that are oppressed...."

In our local church, we realize that God is doing something new. This new thing is a "new baby" that has been born. It still needs nurturing and growth, but now more than ever before I am carrying the heart for the poor. What God wants to do fills my heart to overflowing.

People want to see all kinds of great things happen, but God simply is looking for those who are willing to follow

Him. He wants people to go into the streets and preach the gospel to the poor with dignity and intelligence, not with "craziness." The story of God needs to be conveyed—that God has loved them and has given His life for them.

The Message of Love

The message of God is a message of love. It is a love story of the passion of God. There are hundreds of verses of Scripture that refer to God's love, but there is none better than John 3:16: "For God so loved the world, that He gave His only begotten Son, that whosoever believeth in Him should not perish, but have everlasting life."

The Person Who Loves: The Sovereign

The poor must hear about the Person who loves them. They think God hates them, because they are poor. They think God has discarded and despised them. They need to know that God loves them. When they hear the real gospel, they are going to come to Jesus Christ. Concerning the passion of God, this message of love, the poor need to know that the Person who loves is called the Sovereign.

The Scripture says, "For God so loved the world...." It is important to let the poor know that the Church loves them and Christians love them, but it is most essential to let them know that God loves them. The poor need to know the Person who loves them. They not only need to know the Person who loves (the Sovereign), but they also need to know the possession He loves—the Son.

The Possession He Loves: The Son

God loves so much that He gave up His most prized possession, His Son. How many fathers would sacrifice their only son at God's request? God told Abraham to offer his son on the altar, and Abraham obeyed. How many of us would give up our children or other things to God? There are few things that people give to God, but He gave the possession He loved the most.

God gave for the poor so that they might hear the gospel. In Luke 4:18 Jesus says that the Scripture is fulfilled. He says He is the anointed Messiah and that He is going to preach to the poor. The gospel could not have come to the poor if God had not given up His most loved possession, His own Son.

The only begotten Son of God not only died for the world, but He left the riches of Heaven and entered into poverty upon this earth. He took on all kinds of temptations, problems and situations, so that He might preach the gospel to the poor. God loved so much that He gave up all He had, all He loved, so that the poor might have the gospel preached to them. Even though Jesus came to accomplish that feat, the gospel is not being preached to the poor today!

In the Old Testament God told Moses He was going to destroy all of the people. God said He was going to kill the people and start a new seed from Moses. Moses pleaded and asked God to spare them. Moses' argument was that the whole world would laugh.

Those people whom God wanted to kill were the seed of Abraham, people of covenant. Obviously, there must be a Moses somewhere today, interceding, holding back the hand of God from destroying the Church and starting over, because of its negligence in executing the simplicity of the gospel. Every Christian knows how to quote John 3:16, but few understand the greatest possession of God, His only Son. God gave so that His story of love (the gospel) might be preached to the poor.

The People He Loves: The Sinners

It may seem like a strange paradox, but God loves sinners. He does not love their sins, but He loves them. Throwing the baby out with the bath water is not God's way. He knows how to take the sin from the sinner and separate them in His mind; He can see the difference. God sees the sin, but He looks beyond and sees the sinner. He hates the sin, but He loves the sinner. It is amazing.

In the same way that people have difficulty understanding sinners, they do not understand the poor people. The thing that most people do not realize is that if they were poor, lacking food and shelter, they would act just like the poor street people. Lack and deprivation cause people to behave a certain way.

People make the mistake of criticizing poor people and attributing aspects of poverty to their culture and ethnicity, but the problem of poverty goes much deeper than that. Poverty does not care about your color or the language you speak. It does not discriminate. However, God is the same way—He does not discriminate. There is no exclusivity at the cross of Jesus Christ. God gave up His best, His Son, so that *whosoever* might be saved. In order to give up their greatest possession, most people would have to have some "say so" about who gets it—people want their best possessions to go to special people. But, God is not like that; He gave up that which He loved most so that sinners might be saved.

The Purpose That He Loves: Our Salvation

The reason God loves the poor is that they might be saved. For the same reason, God loves the rich and the middle class. "For God so loved the world, that He gave His only begotten Son, that whosoever believeth in Him should not perish, but have everlasting life" is not only a message of love, but is also a message of liberty.

The Message of Liberty

The message of liberty found in John 3:16 speaks of the power of God. A few years ago, a black pastor from the inner city of Chicago came to me and said, "Dr. Kaufman, anybody who would stay in that neighborhood where you are has to be a man of God." He had been in the Bronx before, and although he lives in a bad neighborhood of Chicago, he had not seen anything like the South Bronx. The brother went on to say, "You have the power of God because you remained there all these years."

Preachers cannot come into the ghetto with a flashy tie, fancy suit and no gospel power. The Church has been talking about a gospel it does not have. It has been talking about a power it does not manifest. The churches are afraid of preaching to the poor, maybe because there is a great need for anointing in order to preach to the poor. People should not think they do not need the anointing. Jesus needed it. If Jesus needed it, we definitely need the anointing.

The Spirit of Christ Is Liberty

In looking at this liberty and power that God gives to the poor, we see that the Spirit of Christ is liberty. "For the law of the Spirit of life in Christ Jesus hath made me free from the law of sin and death" (Rom. 8:2).

There is a Spirit of life that is in Christ. This law of the Spirit of Christ has separated us from the law of sin and death. The law of gravity is similar to the law of sin and death: whatever goes up must come down. When a person throws a handkerchief into the air, it comes down. If that handkerchief is thrown into the air repeatedly, each time it will come down. No matter what is done to the handkerchief, once it is thrown into the air, the law of gravity takes hold of it and makes it come down.

The Bible says we were under the law of sin and death; therefore, we were in the process of "going down." But something interrupted us. It was "the law of the Spirit of life." There is a greater law than the law of sin and death.

Back to the handkerchief illustration: something can be done to stop the law of gravity from taking effect. If someone were to stick out a hand to catch a falling handkerchief, it would stop the effect of the law of gravity. This is what happens to those saved from sin. The law of sin and death was pulling us down, but God "put His hand out and grabbed us." The greater law, the law of Jesus Christ, intercepted the law of sin and death. The thing that people must remember is to stay in the hand of Jesus to keep from falling. Not only is the Spirit of Christ liberty, but the standing in Christ also is liberty.

The Standing in Christ Is Liberty

Liberty is not something obtained and lost. It is something one obtains and keeps. Paul wrote to the Galatian church, "Stand fast therefore in the liberty wherewith Christ hath made us free..." (Gal. 5:1).

We need to stand in Christ. Liberty is not going to church, getting prayed for, leaving church and going out to do the same things that were done before coming to God. Many demon-possessed people have been prayed for and then gone out and involved themselves again with the same activities that led them into demonic possession. When they came back, they had ten more demons than they had before. Other people have gone to an altar, and as soon as they left church, they went right back into that for which they had come for prayer. This is not standing in the liberty that has been afforded us.

People have to go beyond simply getting liberty; they have to stand in that liberty. Imagine someone leaving his air-conditioned bedroom on a day when the weather is 105 degrees. He closes the bedroom door and goes into the kitchen to do some cooking. While there in the hot kitchen, he says, "I don't know why it's so hot. I have the air conditioner on in the bedroom." The statement is true, but the man did not stay in the bedroom.

"Stand fast therefore in the liberty wherewith Christ hath made us free." This is what God wants the poor to do. This can be difficult, because in many instances people in poverty live undisciplined lives. It is one thing to get a poor person into a church building or to an altar, but it is an altogether different thing to teach that person how to live. The Church needs to learn how to help the poor stand fast in the liberty wherewith Christ has set them free, so they will stay in that "air-conditioned bedroom" and not return to the "heat of the kitchen."

The Substitution Is Liberty

Jesus died in our place. This brings us into liberty.

*Therefore if any man be in Christ, he is a new crea-
ture; old things are passed away; behold, all things
are become new... For He hath made Him to be sin
for us, who knew no sin; that we might be made the
righteousness of God in Him.*

II Corinthians 5:17,21

On what do we base our liberty? We base it on the Spirit
of Christ, the standing in Christ and the substitution in
Christ. That same liberty is for the poor. The gospel of Jesus
Christ, the story of God, the good news is for them. We need
to preach it to them.

The Message of Loyalty

The gospel of Jesus Christ is a *message of love*. It is a
message of liberty, but it is also a *message of loyalty*. A person with a close relationship to God can really appreciate His
loyalty. It is something that has become personal in my experience. When my brothers and sisters do not understand, God is
always there. When my wife and children do not understand,
God is there. When confusion sets in, He is there. When the
feeling of loneliness comes, God never leaves. Some have the
impression that preachers are surrounded by people all the
time. This is not true. People leave, and preachers get just as
lonely as anyone else. In fact, they get more lonely because
they give out so much. But, God is always there. He is loyal.

The Purity of God

The message of loyalty speaks of the purity of God. What
makes God pure? For one thing, He is always there—in the

good times and in the bad times. The vows exchanged in wedding ceremonies reflect the relationship of Jesus Christ, the Bridegroom, and the Church, the bride. In wedding vows people profess their love for each other, for better or worse, in sickness and in health. This type of declaration comes from God; He is that way in relation to us. He is there always. God remains true to His people even when they do bad. He does not appreciate the bad, but He is still there. He has said, "I will never leave thee. I will never forsake thee."

Looking closely into the first part of the 49th chapter of Isaiah, one finds that the Israelites were in a city that was destitute. The people had come back from captivity to a desolate land, and they were a people who were despised. Things were going badly.

The city had been destroyed, and the Israelites were what we refer to today as "homeless" and "poor." Because of their condition, they concluded that God had forgotten them.

Sing, O heavens; and be joyful, O earth; and break forth into singing, O mountains: for the Lord hath comforted His people, and will have mercy upon His afflicted. But Zion said, The Lord hath forsaken me, and my Lord hath forgotten me.

Isaiah 49:13-14

The poor in our neighborhoods, cities and country feel this same way, because they are poor. Knowing that some people live in great splendor and opulence, when the poor reflect on their atrocious living conditions, they think that God has forgotten them. How will the poor know that God has not forgotten them, unless God raises up a people to tell them?

In Isaiah 49 there are some interesting things to consider about God. There is "the praise of His being there." The Israelites coming out of captivity were told to sing and praise God, because He knew that He had not forgotten them. It is important to understand the need to praise God for His being there. Do not make the mistake of taking God for granted. We have the tendency to take one another for granted: we take our parents, spouses, jobs, and our education and educators for granted. Then when God says, "Sing," we take Him for granted, and we do not want to sing. The blessing of God has come upon our lives, yet when God wants us to do something, there is resistance. There must be praise because of God's being there.

Also, there is "the promise of His being there." The second part of Isaiah 49:13 says God "...will have mercy upon His afflicted." This is a tremendous promise to the poor: He will have mercy upon them. God is saying this to them in His Word, but God's people are not telling it to them.

Think about what must go through the mind of the average 12-, 13- or 14-year-old from the streets. A lot of them think about how they are going to die. They think they will be beaten up. They think they might get shot. They think about becoming drug addicts or getting AIDS. They think about all of these things, yet there is a promise of God for them. But, no one has been telling them about this promise from God.

There is also "the passion of His being there."

Although men and women are created equal by God, they are not created the same. Men are able to do things that cannot be done by women; women are able to do things that cannot be done by men.

Under most normal circumstances, when a child is tired and is in the presence of both his parents, he goes directly to his mother. His first love affair is with "Mommy." In His description of a love affair, God could use no greater example than the love between a mother and her child: "Can a woman forget her sucking child, that she should not have compassion on the son of her womb? yea, they may forget, yet will I not forget thee" (Isa. 49:15). "Can a woman forget..." speaks of the passion of a mother for her child. The bond of love between a mother and child is very strong during the time of breast-feeding. Many young men are unable to understand, as women do, the love expression that a mother has for a child, because they do not breast-feed. But, God gives His love to us in this same way. The name of God, *El Shaddai*, means "the breast." He nourishes us with His love.

Do the poor know that the passion of God is there? Have they been told of the proof of His being there? Have they been informed of His protection because of His being there—that all of their enemies will scatter? They do not know. Therefore, they do not come to God.

The Message of Life

This message of love speaks of the passion of God; this message of liberty speaks of the power of God; this message of loyalty deals with the purity of God. It is also a message of life that speaks of the purpose of God.

In John 10:9-13 there are four points that can be used to expand on this purpose of God. The center point, in John 10:10, is that one might have life abundantly.

The Access of Life

Looking at verse 9, we see there is the access of life. "I am the door: by Me if any man enter in, he shall be saved, and shall go in and out, and find pasture" (John 10:9). It is not a special man that may enter in. It is not a rich man or an educated man, but any man may enter in. Christ Jesus is God, and He is the Door for any man, so that he "shall go in and out," having the access of life.

The purpose of God is not only access to life, but the abundance of life. "...I am come that they might have life, and that they might have it more abundantly" (John 10:10). Do the poor need to hear that? Do they need to know that life can be more abundant? Do they need to know that the thief comes to steal, kill and destroy, but Jesus came that they might have life and that life more abundantly? Yes, the poor need to hear that.

The Atonement of Life

John 10:11 talks about the atonement for life. The atonement is the work of Jesus Christ on the cross. It is the reconciliation between God and man by which they can once again become one. "I am the Good Shepherd: the Good Shepherd giveth His life for the sheep" (John 10:11). Jesus lives up to that statement. Jesus died so that they might live, but the poor do not know that there is an atonement for their lives.

The Abuse of Life

Let us look at John 10:12-13:

But he that is an hireling, and not the shepherd, whose own the sheep are not, seeth the wolf coming, and leaveth the sheep, and fleeth; and the wolf catcheth them, and scattereth the sheep. The hireling fleeth, because he is an hireling, and careth not for the sheep.

What we have in poverty is the abuse of life, not the atonement. Although this is not doctrine, rather an analogy or illustration, think of the hireling as a drug dealer. The drug dealer is always there when a person has money; but when a person is in trouble and wants to be bailed out of jail, the drug dealer cannot be found. The drug dealer will not sell his gold chain or expensive car to get a person who buys his drugs out of trouble.

People who use drugs will do anything for the drug dealer (or anybody who can feed their drug habit), but the truth is the only One who is there for you when trouble comes is Jesus Christ. He is the only One who will give His life for you.

Jesus is the Great Shepherd who is willing to die for the sheep. He is not like many who are hirelings—they see trouble and they run away. In the streets, people are close to one another until a situation arises in which someone may have to go to jail. Then, all of a sudden, the one who was supposed to be a close friend will do all that he can to avoid going to jail, and he will let you go instead.

Many say there are hypocrites in the Church. Yes, there are. But, the bars and streets are filled with them also. It is not right for a person to come into a church and say it is filled with hypocrites, when he just came out of a city filled with hypocrites. Who in your city will lay down his life for someone? That type of person is very hard to find, but there is Someone who already laid down His life for the world. His Name of Jesus Christ, King of kings and Lord of lords. He is the Great Shepherd. He has given His life for the sheep. He has given His life for the poor.

Paul said, "For me to live is Christ...." That is all! It is not Christ in addition to something else, it is *only* Christ. Paul does not say anything else in that Scripture. He is not saying, "For me to live is Christ and a new suit" or "For me to live is Christ and a new pair of shoes." To live is Christ, because Christ is everything.

The Message of Longsuffering

This message of longsuffering is a demonstration of the patience of God. Where would we be if God had not been patient toward us? God waited a long time for me. Some think God is impatient and He will not wait. Yet, God demonstrates that He is longsuffering.

The Bible says,

The Lord is not slack concerning His promise, as some men count slackness; but is longsuffering to us-ward, not willing that any should perish, but that all should come to repentance.

                                                        II Peter 3:9

In this verse of Scripture we find that God is not willing that *any* should perish. Once again, that eliminates exclusivity. Salvation is not only for the Jews. It is not only for the blacks or the Armenians or the Polish. God does not designate that salvation is specifically for any group of people. He is patiently waiting for everybody to repent.

God is patiently waiting for the poor to repent. The reason they are not repenting is the Church has not been preaching the gospel to them. People cannot repent if they do not hear the gospel.

Take note of three aspects of God's longsuffering.

1. Divine direction
2. Divine devotion
3. Divine delay

God's lovingkindness is pointed directly toward us. This is divine direction. God's divine devotion makes it clear that He is not willing that any should perish. In thinking about divine delay one can readily see that the condition of society could sorely try someone's patience; it is so bad that one might think God should kill everybody. Maybe the angels in Heaven ask God, "Why are you waiting?" Jesus possibly would say, "Because God is longsuffering."

Some people have looked down at the poor and said, "When are they going to get themselves straightened out?" The poor may never get straightened out until we, the Church, get straightened out. God is making a divine delay for them. The people who want to see the poor wiped out, killed, destroyed from the face of the earth or shipped out of this country are going to have to wait. God has set into motion a clock with a divine delay mechanism that will wait until the gospel is preached to the poor. God is not only waiting for them to repent, He is also waiting for us to go out there and preach. God is holding back the winds of judgment until His people go out and take the gospel to the poor.

The Message of Laboring

There is also a message of laboring: the partnership with God.

Come unto Me, all ye that labor and are heavy laden, and I will give you rest. Take My yoke upon you, and learn of Me; for I am meek and lowly in heart: and ye shall find rest unto your souls. For My yoke is easy, and My burden is light.

Matthew 11:28-30

In looking at this word *come* let us consider the call to the weary, the call to the willing and the call to the weakling.

The Call to the Weary

The call to the weary is "Come all ye that are weary and heavy laden." Jesus wants the weary to come to Him. People in deep poverty have a weariness in their lives. For every step a person with money takes to obtain the basic necessities of life, a poor person has to take about 50 steps.

People with money can send someone to the store for them, and middle-class people are able to get into comfortable cars that are heated in the winter and air-conditioned in the summer, drive to the supermarket, shop for groceries, and then take them right to the driveways of their homes. Poor people usually have to walk many blocks to get to a supermarket and then carry very heavy packages for many blocks. They are weary.

The stores where the poor shop have higher prices than the stores of the rich people. This adds another dimension of weariness. The poor are not only weary in body, but they are also weary in their mind, and spirit. They are weary in every way. Basic survival and obtaining three meals a day are challenges of life to the poor. For those who are not poor, it is a great challenge to limit ourselves to three meals a day. Many of us eat too much—all the time. We are able to eat as much as we want, yet, at the same time, there are those who have to search the garbage cans for food. It makes no sense.

The Call to the Weary Worker

The call to the weary worker is rest. Jesus said to all those who were weary and heavy laden, "I will give you rest." The poor are weary of hard labor with little pay. Sometimes the poor spend a lot of time looking for soda cans to get a few dollars. Guys stay out all day wiping windshields only to make a few dollars. Doing that day after day can make a person weary. But, Jesus wants to give them rest.

The Call to the Weary Worshiper

To the weary worshiper He gives refreshment. The poor are weary of religious observances. Poor people tend to be religious because they are trying to find some way to deal with their circumstances. The only thing that is there for them is religion, but it is not the gospel.

Many poor people try to do everything they think will please God. They get candles and/or beads. Some put hats on; some take hats off. They wear this, or they cannot wear that. They wear their hair long (depending on the church), or they wear it short. They make every kind of change in order to observe these religious traditions. It causes them to become very weary, but God gives refreshment to the weary worshiper.

The Call to the Weary Worldling

The weary worldling is a pleasure seeker. People will put much money into the world system looking for pleasure. In Atlantic City people gamble all their money away. Others put money into drugs trying to find a few minutes of pleasure. They go into houses of ill repute trying to find pleasure. At the end of it all, there is emptiness.

In the Bible, the woman at the well had been with all kinds of men, and she still had not found reality and purpose for life. Jesus told her that if she drank of His water, she would never thirst again. After the weary worldling has tried everything, looking for the answer to life, he should come to Jesus.

People are serving God because the world gave them nothing. The world cannot give us the essential things we really need. It is because the world cannot give peace that so many people are on tranquilizers. Although sometimes people have found happiness in the world, they have not found joy. Jesus is the answer for those who are weary of the worldliness.

The Call to the Willing

When Jesus says, "Take My yoke," it necessitates a willingness on our part. The call to the willing is a relationship.

A Relationship With the Lord

Yoke speaks of relationship. When two oxen are yoked together, their heads are placed on either side of the yoke. Jesus is saying that He will place Himself on one side and the other side is for those who are willing to join Him. A relationship develops because of such closeness. Because of the closeness there is an ability to "smell one another's breath." Some have never smelled the breath of God because there is a great distance between them. God did not create the distance, however.

People want to serve God, but they have to come close to Him, they need to get close enough to put their head in the yoke next to Him. A person will not only be close enough to smell God's breath, but he will be able to pull together with God.

In joining a yoke with someone the two people will be pulling in the same direction; they cannot go in two different directions. They need to pull together at the same time. To get into a yoke with Jesus is to get into a yoke with God; that means being willing to work with God.

God is calling the poor into a partnership with Him. God would like the poor to come and share in His work. He wants them to be "a partner in His corporation."

The Relationship by Our Learning

The Scripture says, "Take My yoke upon you." This is the relationship with the Lord. The Scripture goes on to say, "Learn of Me." Jesus will show a person how to pull the cart. One need only to be willing, and Jesus will teach him.

The Relationship While Leaning

God is telling the poor to lean on Him, they do not need to lean on street knowledge or the ability to be slick. God wants them to lean on Him. The message the Church needs to tell the poor is "Lean on God." They might say, "I'm weary." That's okay. Just tell them to put their head on the shoulder of Jesus, get close enough to lean on Him, and the needed relationship will develop.

The Call to the Weakling

In comparison to God everybody is weak. But, when we are weak, He is strong. Jesus says, "My yoke is easy, and My burden is light." The word *easy*, derived from the Greek, means "Profitable." It is profitable for one to allow

Jesus to take part in the yoke he carries. Jesus is willing to share the work load.

The Book of Hebrews tells us to lay aside every weight, yet Jesus said to take His burden. He knows that the burden of the world is impossible, but His burden is possible. Jesus said that when we take His burden, He will lighten the load.

God is not going to put on the poor that which the world puts on the poor. God is not going to allow the poor to be cheated, abused or taken advantage of. His burden is going to be light.

Beware of those who trample on the needy and try to destroy the poor. The Scripture says,

We can hardly wait for the holy days to be over so that we can sell our grain. When will the Sabbath end, so that we can start selling again? Then we can overcharge, use false measures, and fix the scales to cheat our customers. We can sell worthless wheat at a high price. We will find a poor man who cannot pay his debts, not even the price of a pair of sandals, and we will buy him as a slave.

Amos 8:4-6 (Good News Bible)

The world makes people into slaves, but God saves us. His burden is light.

Chapter Two

The Medicine for the Poor

...He hath sent me to heal the brokenhearted....

Luke 4:18

Preaching on this topic was like preaching to a stone wall. It was not "preaching over someone's head," it was more like "preaching over someone's *heart.*" When one preaches over people's heads, they simply do not understand. When one preaches over people's hearts, there is a resistance, because they don't want to accept it.

In order to minister to the poor, we must understand the heart of God. Hearts have to be lifted up to receive His heart. Preaching down to people's hearts will dilute the message. The message to the poor has already been diluted for such a long time. Resistance is no reason to stop preaching this message, although the temptation to do so exists.

I am hopeful that in reading this the reader will be encouraged to lift his heart to God and say, "I want to be like David." With all of David's weaknesses and frailties, he was a man after God's own heart. He wanted the things God wanted. He loved the things God loved. David loved the people God loved. How can one be a Christian and not be a person after God's heart?

The Bible contains the heart of God. Christians sing about having Jesus in their hearts, yet when someone preaches the heart of God, we cannot rise to the occasion. When we get the heart of God, we will soon see the hand of God reaching out with His power. God will give to us perception to see in revelation what others who are saved cannot see. We will be able to feel through the heart of God.

It is important to love what God loves and the people He loves. No matter how one tries, one could never get close to God in any other way. We must understand that God is the God of the poor, and we are going to have to be people after God's heart. This will cause us to care for the poor.

One of the greatest problems the poor have is what our text calls "a broken heart." People in deep poverty have broken hearts. This type of poverty is not just a poverty in which a person does not have money. It is the kind in which people are so poor that nobody cares for them; they are brokenhearted as a result of being poor. Many are brokenhearted because they are not able to eat and they have no shelter.

There is a paradox associated with poverty and brokenheartedness: some are poor as a result of having a broken heart. When one has a broken heart, he has no desire to get up and go on; therefore, he stops functioning. He no longer has the zeal to work, and eventually, poverty sets in. Having a broken heart can lead people into poverty, and being poor causes people to have broken hearts. Thus, poverty and a broken heart are closely interrelated.

Ministry to the poor deals with healing their broken hearts. We will cover these three areas:

1. Their despair, "...the brokenhearted...."
2. The declaration, "...to heal [or to bind]...."
3. The direction, "...He hath sent Me...."

Their Despair

To get a better understanding of the type of despair that plagues the lives of those in poverty, let us look at the real meaning of *brokenhearted*. We will look at both the Hebrew and Greek definitions because in Luke 4:18 Jesus quotes Isaiah 61:1, which was written in Hebrew.

In both Hebrew and Greek the words *broken* and *hearted* are two clearly distinct words. The Hebrew word for *broken* means "to burst; to break; to crush; to destroy; to hurt; to quench; and to tear." The Hebrew word for *heart* means "the feelings; the will; the intellect; and the center of everything."

Luke 4:18 was written in Greek. *Broken* in Greek means "to crush completely; to shatter; to break into pieces; to break into slivers, and to bruise." The Greek word for *heart* means "the feelings, the mind, the middle or center of anything."

Putting these meanings together, we see that to be *brokenhearted* means that the very center of someone's being— his intellect, feelings and will—is hurt, broken, crushed, destroyed, torn apart and quenched.

We speak of having a broken heart due to a bad love affair, and this is one area. If the relationship was intense, a person's heart, feelings, thoughts, emotions and will are broken. Their whole life seems crushed, and it seems as though all is lost.

The brokenheartedness one may feel when he receives 87 percent on a test rather than 91 percent is different from that of someone whose will is utterly destroyed. Sometimes brokenheartedness reaches a point at which a person's feelings and thought processes are entirely destroyed. He is unable to feel "right." He cannot think in the right way. He stops acting as he ought to act.

Jesus said that God sent Him to these people. This is the heart of God. He wants to rebuild lives. He wants to put shattered hearts together. In Isaiah 61 the word is *to bind.* Putting hearts together is a healing process. When a bone is broken, the natural process used to heal the bone is to push it back together and "set" it.

People who are brokenhearted need to be healed for several reasons:

Their Happiness Is Gone

A person who is brokenhearted has no happiness. They have no joy. There is nothing that they rejoice over. Nothing seems to excite them. Jesus was sent to bind them up so they could have joy and release their emotions.

Their Hope Is Gone

A brokenhearted person feels that all hope is gone. Hope resides in the heart, will and feelings. So when a person is brokenhearted, his mind, will and feelings are gone. He feels as though there is no hope for tomorrow.

Imagine what it would be like to live with no hope for tomorrow. School children have hope that June will come and school will be over. Teachers have hope that June will come and the children will be gone. Parents have hope that one day their children will leave home and go out on their own. Employees have hope of receiving a week's salary; this is the excitement of the working man. This is his hope. Just about everybody has hope, But, what hope is there for a poor child when June comes and school closes, and he is no longer able to receive regular meals for the entire summer? What hope does a nonworking person have when payday never comes for him?

Their Health Is Gone

A person whose will, feelings and mind are gone eventually becomes physically sick. There is no doubt that when a person is not well mentally, he will not be well physically, he will not be able to properly take care of his body.

Their Harmony Is Gone

When there is harmony, there is peace; everything coincides and things fit into their proper place. When a band plays in harmony, it is beautiful; every sound is intact. On the other hand, if each member of the band would play a different song, key or tempo, it would sound awful. Some people's lives are that way.

Their Help Is Gone

Our greatest help comes from God, but the brokenhearted do not have Him in the midst of their brokenness. Outside the spiritual realm, our greatest help comes from within ourselves; there is an ability to find enough inner strength to do what could not normally be done, and at times of need, help arises from within. But, when a person is brokenhearted, that does not happen.

Their Home Is Gone

Why are so many people homeless today? Not everybody who is homeless is out of his mind. Not all of the homeless are so poor that they cannot afford to live somewhere. Some are educated, and some have what they need to get housing, yet they are homeless. Why?

One reason, but not the only reason, is some are so brokenhearted that they no longer have the capacity to work, earn a salary, pay rent or have a checking account. They just cannot do those things. So, what happens? They lose their homes because they are not able to perform the simplest tasks.

In many instances, if they were to have a home, they would not take care of it. They would not scrub the floor, wash the dishes or cook for themselves. Because they are so shattered, they eat out of garbage cans. We look at them and think it is disgusting. Although we may not realize it, we are only seeing an effect, not a cause. These people are brokenhearted, and Jesus came to earth for them.

Their Heart Is Gone

The heart is that which propels people. It is the heart that makes people take a chance to go for an interview for a job for which they do not think they are qualified. We say, they have "heart"; in Yiddish it is called "chutzpa" ("guts" or boldness).

Why do some people have no heart? Because it has been shattered, broken, destroyed and stepped on. It is gone. This is the despair of the brokenhearted.

The Declaration

Jesus did not come just to let us know that there are brokenhearted people or to let the world know there are brokenhearted people in society. He made a declaration that they are there and He has come to heal them.

Jesus came to bind up those broken hearts. He came to put the shattered pieces together as the potter had remade the vessel in Jeremiah 18. When Jesus stood up and quoted Isaiah 61, He declared to the people in the synagogue that He had come to heal.

It is the will of God for the brokenhearted to be healed. Some people like to lick their wounds; however, they need to allow Jesus to bind up those wounds. Some have carried hurts all of their lives. Their hearts have been crushed, and they have never let God heal them completely.

Jesus may have healed some wounds in the hearts of those who have been saved, but there also are some wounds that have not been healed. For instance, there are women who have trouble with men because of incidents with their fathers. Some earthly fathers have not been such good guys, but our Heavenly Father is an excellent Father.

God not only "mends fences," He mends minds, He mends feelings and wills. He is able to take that which is broken and make it whole again. He can cause a person to become the man or woman of God that He wants them to be, because He is able to heal their broken heart.

The declaration of God is that He came so that the brokenhearted might be healed. He has come to heal them and to bind up their wounds. He has come to make them a new creature. Jesus has come so that the brokenhearted might live and have feelings once again. He came so that they might seek life and that their will might be revived.

How are the brokenhearted healed?

The Brokenhearted Are Healed by His Passion

Hebrews 4:15 says, "For we have not an high priest which cannot be touched with the feelings of our infirmities...." Jesus is touched with the hurt of the brokenhearted, because of His great love. He is such a loving God that He can be touched with our feelings, hurts, broken emotions, broken-down wills and broken-down minds. Jesus is touched by that. The brokenhearted are healed by His passion.

The Brokenhearted Are Healed by His Person

Isaiah 53:4 says, "Surely He hath borne our griefs, and carried our sorrows...." It is obvious that in dealing with the brokenhearted Jesus was dealing with sorrows. The Hebrew definition of the word *carry* means "to bear a burden." There is a difference between carrying an attaché case and carrying a burden. In His person, Jesus carried our burdens and sorrows. While He was on the cross, He took our sorrows and our broken hearts. They are able to be healed. Anything Jesus took to the cross can be healed. Broken hearts are able to be healed because He took them onto His person.

The Brokenhearted Are Healed by His Promise

Hosea 6:1 says, "Come, and let us return unto the Lord: for He hath torn, and He will heal us; He hath smitten, and He will bind us up." What is the promise? If a person goes to the Lord, He will bring the healing and bind them up. When God says all of His promises are "yea" and "amen," He means it.

The Brokenhearted Are Healed by His Power

Acts 10:38 says, "How God anointed Jesus of Nazareth with the Holy Ghost and with power: who went about doing good, and healing all that were oppressed of the devil; for God was with Him." Jesus went about with the power that God had given Him. What was Jesus doing? He was doing good. We are healed of our hurts by His power.

The Direction

In the New Testament Jesus speaks of being sent by the Father. Jesus did not say a denomination sent Him. He did not say a board of ruling elders sent Him. He did not even say a group of people who took an offering sent Him. He said, "My Father hath sent me."

God sent Jesus to the poor, the afflicted and everybody else. In these last days, many seem to think that God sends Jesus only to the rich. Some preach that Jesus Himself was rich while He was here on earth. Some preach that His disciples had a lot of money. This is very interesting, for in the Book of Acts, when the lame man asked for money, Peter said, "Silver and gold have I none...." Either Peter was a liar, or he did not have any money.

Jesus was sent and directed to the poor. At one point He told John the Baptist, "...The poor have the gospel preached to them." He was saying that He was Messiah, because no one else was preaching the gospel to the poor, except He.

Jesus did not come to earth without being sent. He said, "I am sent by My Father." The biblical pattern of releasing is from father to son: from God, the Father, to Jesus, His Son. The Father told Jesus to go and Jesus obeyed. When He came to earth, men challenged Him. They asked Him what He was doing here, and Jesus said, "My Father sent Me." He was not here on His own. He had a mission to accomplish. Jesus was never afraid to be challenged about anything He did, because He knew God had sent Him. This is powerful! When God sent Jesus, He gave Him something to enable Him to accomplish the task. Jesus was empowered by the Father. With that empowerment, Jesus approached the poor.

Jesus Came to the Poor With a Divine Approach

Matthew 12:18-21 says,

Behold My Servant, whom I have chosen; My Beloved, in whom My soul is well pleased: I will put My Spirit upon Him, and He shall show judgment to the Gentiles. He shall not strive, nor cry; neither shall any man hear His voice in the streets. A bruised reed shall He not break, and smoking flax shall He not quench, till He send forth judgment unto victory. And in His name shall the Gentiles trust.

His Approach Is Tactful

The divine approach Jesus used was tactful. Verse 19 of the above Scripture says, "He shall not strive, nor cry; neither shall any man hear His voice in the streets." This does not mean that Jesus would not preach in the streets. That is not what God is talking about. The word *strive* really means "to be quarrelsome." So, in essence, God is saying that He did not send His Son to strive and be quarrelsome. God has not sent His Son to fight with the poor, rather He sent Jesus to feed the poor.

Likewise God has not sent us to fight with the poor. Our country is at war with the poor; they are cursing the poor, and the poor are already cursed. What the poor in our country need is for the Church, the people who know God, to stand up for them, love them and care for them. This is not to say that the Church needs to pamper the poor, but God's love must be expressed to them through us.

Many people are poor today because of some of the churches. The churches have not lent a helping hand and lifted up a soul, unless the hand they were lifting had money in it.

The approach to the poor should be tactful. Do not be cheated by the poor. Do not be abused by connivers. On the other hand, while dealing with honest poor people, be tactful. There are enough people bothering them, they do not need any more abuse.

His Approach Is Tender

Jesus' approach is not only tactful, but it is also tender. Verse 20 of Matthew 12 says, "A bruised reed shall He not break, and smoking flax shall He not quench, till He send forth judgment unto victory." The reed speaks of feebleness, and a bruised reed is an emblem of the poor and oppressed. Reeds are delicate; they are bruised without much effort. There are people who break things that are already bruised. Why? Because they feel bigger when they stand on top of someone. Jesus did not come to conquer the poor. He wins their hearts with His love.

Matthew 12:20 also speaks of the smoking flax. This refers to the wick of the lamp when the oil is exhausted. The flame is about to die out, and there is hardly any light left. Some people are like that. Their lives are like flickering flames, then someone comes along to put out the little bit of light that is left in their lives.

Instead of putting out the light in people's lives, Jesus pours in the oil, trying to keep the flame lit. In order to be godly and Christlike, we must not put out others' lights, rather we need to pour on the oil.

His Approach Was Trusting

Not only was Jesus' divine approach tactful and tender, but it was trusting. Matthew 12:21 says, "And in His name shall the Gentiles trust." The Gentiles were the outsiders, those to whom the gospel was not preached at that time. It is amazing that the gospel of Matthew, written to the Jews, states that the Gentiles will trust in Jesus.

The poor do not trust Jesus, because they do not know who He is. No one has told them. The Body of Christ is so busy telling one another, we have forgotten the poor. Yet, Jesus can be trusted by the poor. Jesus will never oppress them.

Jesus Came to the Poor With a Divine Authority

Jesus was sent under the authority of the One who sent Him. When someone is sent on a mission, he carries the authority of the sender. Jesus came under divine authority. God, who sent Him, gave Jesus the power to fulfill what God had called Him to do.

Let us look at these four areas of Jesus' divine authority:

1. Divine position
2. Divine provision
3. Divine power
4. Divine anointing

Divine Position

Hebrews 1:1-3 says,

God, who at sundry times and in divers manners spake in time past unto the fathers by the prophets, hath in these last days spoken unto us by His Son, whom He hath appointed heir of all things, by whom also He made the worlds; who being the brightness of His glory, and the express image of His person, and upholding all things by the word of His power, when He had by Himself purged our sins, sat down on the right hand of the Majesty on high....

When Jesus comes to the poor, His position is one of authority. He is the One who sits at the right hand of God.

Divine Provision

For those who are hungry, Jesus is the Bread of Life. For those in darkness, He is the Light of Life. Jesus is everything we need. In John 6:35-40 Jesus says,

...I am the bread of life: he that cometh to Me shall never hunger; and he that believeth on Me shall never thirst. But I said unto you, That ye also have seen Me, and believe not. All that the Father giveth Me shall come to Me; and him that cometh to Me I will in no wise cast out. For I came down from heaven, not to do Mine own will, but the will of Him that sent Me... that of all which He hath given Me I should lose nothing, but should raise it up again at the last day. And this is the will of Him that sent Me, that every one which seeth the Son, and believeth on

Him, may have everlasting life: and I will raise him
up at the last day.

Jesus is our provision. He is the Bread of Life. Jesus is
the very essence of those who are hungry.

Divine Power

With a divine approach, Jesus uses a divine authority to
come to the poor. He is strong when He comes. He comes
under authority, yet He comes with affection, tactfulness,
tenderness and trustfulness. John 9:1-5 says,

And as Jesus passed by, He saw a man which was
blind from his birth. And His disciples asked Him,
saying, Master, who did sin, this man, or his parents,
that he was born blind? Jesus answered, Neither hath
this man sinned, nor his parents: but that the works
of God should be made manifest in him. I must work
the works of Him that sent Me, while it is day: the
night cometh, when no man can work. As long as I
am in the world, I am the Light of the world.

Whether He is the Bread of Life or the Light of the
World, the emphasis is not on who Jesus is, but on who sent
Him. Jesus said, "I am the Bread of Life," but He also said,
"He sent Me." Jesus said, "I am the Light of the world," but
He also said, "He sent Me." The authority (power) to be the
Bread of Life and the Light to shine in the midst of darkness
came to Jesus from God who sent Him.

Divine Anointing

Jesus came to the poor with a divine anointing (the
power of God, the anointing of the Spirit of God). He said,

"the Spirit of the Lord is upon Me, because He hath anointed Me to preach the gospel to the poor...." Concerning anointing, Acts 10:38 and Luke 4:18 speak first of God's presence and secondly of God's power. Acts 10:38 says, "How God anointed Jesus of Nazareth with the Holy Ghost and with power...." Luke 4:18 says, "The Spirit of the Lord is upon Me, because He hath anointed Me...."

God put that authority and power on Jesus. The word *anointing* means "pouring oil." Jesus gave description to the type of oil that was poured on Him when He said that God anointed Him with the Holy Ghost and that the Spirit of the Lord anointed Him. With that anointing Jesus was able to operate by the power of God.

The anointing in Acts 10:38 and Luke 4:18 speaks not only of God's presence and power, but it also speaks of God's purpose. Acts 10:38 also says Jesus went about doing good and healing all who were oppressed of the devil. That was His purpose.

Luke 4:18 says,

The Spirit of the Lord is upon Me [His presence], *because He hath anointed Me* [His power], *to preach the gospel to the poor; He hath sent Me to heal the brokenhearted, to preach deliverance to the captives, and recovering of sight to the blind, to set at liberty them that are bruised* [His purpose]...."

The anointing of God is given to people for a purpose. Some preachers have the problem of wanting to be anointed, just to be anointed, with no purpose. Jesus had a purpose, and the power He had enabled Him to do good and heal those who were oppressed.

The poor people's despair is their brokenheartedness. The declaration is that God has come to heal. The direction is that Jesus was sent by His Father with a divine approach, divine authority and divine anointing to reach the poor.

Chapter Three

The Miracle for the Poor

The Spirit of the Lord is upon Me, because He hath anointed Me to preach the gospel to the poor; He hath sent Me to heal the brokenhearted, to preach deliverance to the captives, and recovering of sight to the blind, to set at liberty them that are bruised [oppressed], to preach the acceptable year of the Lord.

Luke 4:18-19

In this chapter, let us pay attention to the phrase, "to preach deliverance to the captives." The word *preach* is repeated several times in this verse of Scripture. Although each time it appears to be the same word in English, there are two different meanings in Greek.

The first Greek word, in the statement "to preach the gospel to the poor," is *euaggelizo*, meaning "to announce good news" (from it comes the word *evangelize*, especially concerning the gospel). It also means "to declare or bring glad tidings." Thus, it refers to preaching with an evangelistic thrust. *Euaggelizo* is an announcement of good news, declaring happiness because God has come down in Christ Jesus. Looking very closely, one can see that God said it is glad news. Specifically, it is good news to the poor, because they had no good news. It is as though God were saying, "You do not have any good news, but I have come to announce some good news to you, even you who are poor."

The second Greek word, in the phrase "to preach deliverance to the captives," is *Kerusso*. It means to "herald, especially divine truth." It also means "to proclaim, to publish, to herald as a public choir." So, we may say one definition of *to preach* is "the speaking forth of an evangelistic type of good news," and the other is "a public proclamation of something that has happened or is happening."

When the Scripture says, "...to preach deliverance...," it means "to make a public proclamation that God has come to set the captives free." Therefore, in the New International Version it says, "...to proclaim freedom for the prisoner...." In the New American Standard version it says, "...to proclaim release to the captives...." The Good News Bible says, "...to proclaim liberty to the captives...." A little word study helps us to understand.

When interpreting Scripture, one must do so not only in its Greek or Hebrew setting, but also in the historical context. The problems the Greeks were experiencing and their mind set during those days make a difference in the meaning of Scripture. The word *deliverance* from the Greek *aphesis* means "freedom, pardon, deliverance, forgiveness, liberty and remission." Let us look at the word *pardon* in conjunction with *captives*. When God dealt with captives, He was dealing with people who were in prison. This portion of Scripture is saying that Jesus came to preach the good news, and yes, He was sent by God to heal the broken-hearted, but He had also come to proclaim pardon to the prisoners.

It is interesting that the words *pardon* and *prisoners* correlate. If someone tells a prisoner about pardon, he does not need even an elementary education to be able to understand what it means. Pardon is not being set free at the end of one's prison sentence; when a person is pardoned, he is released immediately. Therefore, pardon not only sets one free from prison, but it also sets one free from the penalty of the crime that caused one to be imprisoned. Jesus came to proclaim pardon to the prisoners. He said that He had come to proclaim pardon so people could be released from that which holds them captive.

Jesus not only sets people free from an effect, but also from a cause. He not only sets people free from prison, but also from the penalty. He came to free people from that which brought them into bondage. This is the difference between God's deliverance and the secular understanding of deliverance. Those in the world can help a drug addict to get off drugs, but they cannot forgive sins.

When a man is saved, not only is he set free from the prison of drugs, but he is also set free from the penalty of drug use. This is not merely denominational terminology coined by deliverance ministries. Deliverance is veritable, but there is much more to it than having a sick person healed. When physical healing is all that takes place and the sin-sick soul is not healed, the sickness comes back. So when Jesus says *deliverance*, He means a total setting free from prison. Prison does not have to mean metal bars in a jail cell; it could be crack, lust or something else.

Lust does not necessarily have to pertain to something sexual. Lust is any strong desire that overpowers a person. Some people live in the deepest bondages because they lust after things they cannot have. As a result, they are never happy with life. They see what others have, and they want it badly. They do not want to work for it, and they are too afraid to steal for it, so they live miserable lives, because they never have what they want. This is in total contrast to dreaming a dream of God. It is lusting after something that is not from God.

Having considered the different meanings of several terms, it becomes clear that deliverance to the poor is a proclamation. In fact, it is a public cry from Jesus to everyone. Because it was a proclamation, it was public; being public, it was for everyone; because it was for everyone, it included the poor. In Jesus' day, the poor were always excluded, but Jesus by proclamation included everybody.

Jesus is not merely the Light of God preaching good news, nor is He merely the Love of God being sent to heal the brokenhearted, but He is also the Liberator proclaiming to all those who are bound that He came to set them free. Jesus has proclaimed and is proclaiming that He has come to set men free. God is proclaiming pardon to all who are captives. He is releasing people from their prisons. He will open up the prisons and forgive the past. God sets people free and looses them from that which had them bound. No one has to remain the way they were. Some people think,

"That's not for me." Yes, it is! It is a proclamation. Jesus came to proclaim in all the world pardon to the prisoners.

There are five considerations in the deliverance Jesus proclaimed:

1. Deliverance from the pit of sin
2. Deliverance from the power of satan
3. Deliverance from our painful shackles
4. Deliverance from our passionate seductions
5. Deliverance from our past sinfulness

Deliverance From the Pit of Sin

Psalm 40:2 says, "He brought me up also out of an horrible pit, out of the miry clay...." This is deliverance from the pit of sin. In this verse of Scripture David describes the condition, the pit, and he tells of his twofold deliverance: deliverance not only from the miry clay, but also from the horrible pit. The horrible pit is called "the guilt of sin."

In Hebrew being brought out of a horrible pit meant to be brought up out of a pit of noise. Pits were dug to catch animals, and they were shaped in such a way that sound reverberated. There was screeching in those pits. In this portion of Scripture David is referring to the pits that were dug to capture wolves, bears and lions. Occasionally, thieves and robbers also were trapped that way. The pit was so shaped that every cry for help would echo and reverberate. A trap of this kind was truly a pit of noise. Imagine what it would be like to be caught in a pit where a scream for help caused that noise to echo a loud, screeching sound. It would be torture, but sin is like that.

When people sin, the guilt of sin is ever present. People can "hear the screech" of what they are doing all of the time. They cannot sleep. This is why the world is in turmoil. The Bible says, "...He giveth His beloved sleep," because the noise of guilt is not from God.

To be awakened at night by the sound of a car siren that continuously wails is very annoying, so it's easy to imagine what that pit was like. This is what sin is like, yet Jesus Christ pardons us. Deliverance is pardon. People cannot be set free from the "noise," unless they are forgiven, because the noise represents the guilt due to sin. However, when people are delivered from the pit, they not only have freedom from the pit itself, but they also have freedom from the noise—the guilt and the sin that is in their lives. This is the great thing about Jesus—He does not deal with exteriors, He deals with totalities.

David said in Psalm 32:5, "...I said, I will confess my transgressions unto the Lord; and Thou forgavest the iniquity of my sin." This expresses a deliverance from the guilt of sin (forgiveness), but there is also a deliverance from the grip of sin. "He brought me up...out of the miry clay...." The bottom of those pits often were covered with a sticky sediment which impeded all attempts to escape. In other words, it was not quicksand, but a mudlike clay. The more a person tried to get out by himself, the more the pit held him. The more we try to get out of sin, the more difficult it becomes.

Adam and Eve are a good example of people who became caught in the grip of sin. They tried to cover their sin. Although their bodies were covered, they still were running from God. If their covering had been adequate, there would not have been a need for them to hide. The reason the covering was not adequate is that it was man-made. We can never cover up our own sins. Only God can deliver or pardon us from sin. The more the victim struggles to get free from the "pit," the more he sinks.

When we consider guilt, we talk about forgiveness, but when we consider the grip of sin, we talk about freedom. So the phrase *delivering the captives* speaks of forgiveness and freedom. To be set free from drugs yet have the guilt from past activities hanging over one's head would cause that person to go back to drugs. But, God does a complete work, so a person never has to go back, so people will be set free.

If we are to be freed from the miry clay, it must be by an outside force. We can never be delivered, pardoned or loosed from the prisons and the shackles of our lives without help from Almighty God.

Deliverance From the Power of Satan

There is not only deliverance from the pit of sin, but there is also deliverance from the power of satan. It is time that the Church begin to understand some of these things. The Church does not want to deal with people who are deep in sin. We do not want to bring them in and set them free. The reason for that is we do not want to deal with satan. We would rather deal with nice things. However, we need to let the "wind" blow in order to quench the stench in the streets. We also need deliverance from the power of satan.

In Acts 26:14-18 Paul testifies of his conversion experience and of the words Jesus spoke to him in reference to his call. "...To open their eyes, and to turn them from darkness to light, and from the power of Satan unto God..." (Acts 26:18). There is no doubt that satan has power, but his power is nothing compared to the power of God. The apostle John said, "...greater is He that is you, than he that is in the world" (I John 4:4). However, when God is not in us working that which is well pleasing in His sight, we are under the power and domination of satan.

Satan Is a Hypocrite

There is a familiar phrase spoken of the Church: "There are hypocrites in church." Yes, that is true, because in a sense, satan is in the church, and he is the greatest hypocrite of all. Satan is a first-class liar, and he is the father of all lies.

A lot of people do not know the difference between God's voice and satan's voice. Second Corinthians 11:14 says, "...for satan himself is transformed into an angel of light." He appears to be some nice person, but he is the devil. Genesis 3:4 says, "And the serpent said unto the woman, Ye shall not surely die...." She listened to the serpent, and she died spiritually. We read this and are inclined to say that the woman was stupid, but then we listen to him also. Aren't we stupid? We listen to Satan because he appears as an angel of light, and we are not astute enough to recognize him. We do not check for "fingerprints on the doorknob," so to speak.

Sometimes we do not check because the devil tells us the things we like to hear. We find people saying, "God called me, and nobody understands it." When God has something for a person to do, every devil in hell cannot stop it, unless the person lets him.

"...there is no truth in him. When he speaketh a lie, he speaketh of his own: for he is a liar, and the father of it" (John 8:44). People need to read this verse about twice a day and realize that satan is a hypocrite!

Satan Hates

There is no place in Scripture where divine truth states that satan loves. Satan hates! People need to get that into their hearts and minds. The devil hates people. He has come to seek and destroy people.

Satan hates God's purposes. "...I will build My church; and the gates of hell shall not prevail against it" (Matt. 16:18). Satan hates the Church, especially the Church that is hearing God and knocking down the gates of hell. The devil just hates it!

Satan not only hates God's purpose, but he also hates God's people. The Lord, speaking to Simon Peter, says, "...Satan hath desired to have you, that he may sift you as wheat" (Luke 22:31). God wants to form, strengthen and build people. He wants to bless and use them. God wants to deliver people, and satan wants to destroy them. This is why we need to be so conscious and aware.

People cannot be delivered if they are letting satan rule their lives. In our church, demon-possessed people are set free, only to come in the next Sunday demon-possessed once again. Why? Because they went out and did the same thing they were doing before they came to church. People cannot come to church, be set free from drugs and go out and start using drugs again. People tend to think something mystical is going to happen at the altar, but after a while, it seems that no matter how long we pray for these people, they remain bound. It almost makes no sense to pray for them, because he will come back into their lives in an hour or two.

The devil hates people, and he wants to control them. Sometimes newspaper articles report stories of demon-possessed people who are naked, screaming and screeching in caves. If people do not want this to happen in their life, they had better stay away from satan. People ought to live in the freedom of God. "If the Son therefore shall make you free, ye shall be free indeed" (John 8:36). God does not set people free to go back to satan. The devil will sift them.

Satan Hinders

"Wherefore we would have come unto you, even I Paul, once and again; but Satan hindered us" (I Thess. 2:18). If the great apostle Paul said satan hindered him, who do people think they are saying, "satan cannot hinder me"?

People need to persevere, to "...press toward the mark for the prize of the high calling of God in Christ Jesus" (Phil. 3:14). People should not give up, even when that "quitting" feeling is there.

Every long distance runner has, at some point, felt like stopping. If a person does a lot of swimming, he may go to the pool thinking he can do 50 laps. The first 10 may seem easy. But, while going from lap 10 to 30, he might say, "I'll just do 25 laps today and rest." Then he pushes through, all the way to 30 laps. Again he pushes and reaches 32 laps. He goes all the way to 34 laps, and a new wind comes into him.

The more he presses, the more he pushes. He becomes more determined and goes all the way to 50 laps.

Sometimes, however, people never make it because it is so easy to give up, and satan is trying to stop us. He is working at it, but just as he is persevering, we also need to persevere.

Satan hinders by suggesting doubts. If satan can make people doubt Jesus, he will stop them. If he can make people doubt the vision of the church, he will put them on the sidelines. If he can make people doubt that there is such a thing as spiritual authority, then he will hinder those people.

Satan not only hinders by suggesting doubts, but he also hinders people by starting difficulties. He puts difficulties along the path, and people feel they cannot surmount the hurdles and obstacles, so they decide to sit down for a while. But, they need to persevere.

Suggesting doubts and starting difficulties is not the only way satan hinders. He also sends distractions. This is the biggest problem in Christian life—distractions.

One distraction for young Christians is relationships. One should not be void of relationships throughout his life, but it is very important to be single-minded during the first stage of your Christian walk. A person can only have one love affair at a time. Some people think they are great when they have ten love affairs, but they are not really having love affairs, they just are having sexual experiences. When a person comes to Christ, he needs to fall in love with Jesus 100 percent and cultivate that relationship. To many people this is even more difficult than it sounds, because they never have had relationships in their lives. Then they come to God whom they cannot see, and they want to have a relationship. They do not know how to have a good relationship with God, so it is going to take a while to learn.

Only after one has cultivated a relationship with God can he even begin to get a twinkle in his eye about starting a relationship with someone of the opposite sex. There are people who started out right with God, but are in the world today because they sought relationships with all kinds of men and women before their relationship with God was cultivated. There is nothing worse for a new convert's Christian development than being distracted by someone of the opposite sex. It is not needed. The person may say, "I need a relationship," but he does not need that relationship, yet. He needs a relationship with God first. Satan will give some men the prettiest women in the world, just to turn them from God. These guys know that they are not so good looking that they should be getting such pretty girls. They need to find out why those pretty girls have an eye for them.

In one instance, shortly after a man was saved, a girl who looked like a Hollywood star was in love with him and bought cologne for him. It was because the guy was a young Christian. At one time in his Christian walk, that man had been a baby in the Lord and had to be held in a preacher's arms, carried through and given good advice. Once a person gets past that stage, and he has grown in the Lord and his relationship with God is going well, it may be okay to date, become engaged and marry.

Other distractions for Christians are great jobs, great professions and education that keeps students away from church. People become so engrossed with these things that they have no time for their family, prayer, church, the Word of the Lord or anything else. Yet, these people think they are going to be something great.

Education is important and something to be sought after, but when a person becomes so educated that he thinks he does not need God, it has been a disservice to him. Education without God equals nothing but distractions. After they finish school and get a good job, many go after that big house, and they forget about God.

Some of the greatest distractions are children, families and jobs. These are good things, yet they give us so many problems and trials that they interfere with our relationship with God, and some of us become overwhelmed. A person may have been saved for 80 years, but there still will be distractions.

When people become so bothered by the things of life, they need to come to church. But, many choose to stay away from church when they are dealing with their situations, rather than come to the house of God to hear Him and be released from their problems. Thus, they become more overwhelmed. Next Sunday comes, and they are too overcome to go to church. These distractions are sent by satan; he is the distractor.

Satan Holds Onto Us

Satan holds onto us like strong glue. "And ought not this woman, being a daughter of Abraham, whom Satan hath bound, lo, these eighteen years, be loosed from this bond on the sabbath day?" (Luke 13:16) People think that when satan gets hold of them he is going to let them go the following week. This is an illusion. Some say, "I'm just going to try this once," "I'm just going to sleep with that person once," or "I'll just get high one more time." But, when satan takes hold of a person, he binds him and never wants to let go.

Satan Is Going to Hell

"And cast him [satan] into the bottomless pit, and shut him up, and set a seal upon him, that he should deceive the nations no more..." (Rev. 20:3).

Deliverance From Our Painful Shackles

"If the Son therefore shall make you free, ye shall be free indeed" (John 8:36). We need to understand the liberty that God has given us. We need to understand this deliverance, pardon or proclamation that God has given about setting us free. He pardoned us and forgave us when He set us free from our prisons. God wants to bring us into liberty. "For the law of the Spirit of life in Christ Jesus hath made me free from the law of sin and death" (Rom. 8:2).

People are captives because there is a law of sin and death holding them. The law of the Spirit of life, the Spirit of Christ, is the only thing strong enough to break the law of death. Only the Spirit of life can reach out His hand, take a person from under the law of death and set him free.

Some say, "My children believe in truth, and they live by truth. After all, the Bible is simply man's interpretation." What is the truth that people conjure up in their own minds? Surely, that is man's interpretation. Yet, people come to their own conclusion of what truth is, and they live by that.

A group may get together and say truth is beating up the smallest guy in the pack. Some may say truth is smoking marijuana; they say it brings them closer to God. They used to say that about LSD, and all it did was mess up their brains. The Bible says, "You shall know the truth." Truth is in the Word of God.

God has given a liberty of the Spirit, a liberty of the Savior and a liberty of the Scriptures, because there needs to be a liberty of the saints. "...because the creature itself also shall be delivered from the bondage of corruption into the glorious liberty of the children of God" (Rom. 8:21). There is a liberty of the saints into which God's people may enter. A classic verse of Scripture says, "Therefore if any man be in Christ, he is a new creature: old things are passed away; behold, all things are become new" (II Cor. 5:17).

Deliverance From Our Passionate Seductions

The Person Who Tempts Us

We are seduced and tempted daily. People should not feel belittled because they are tempted. Jesus was tempted.

Now the serpent was more subtle than any beast of the field which the Lord God had made. And he said unto the woman, Yea, hath God said, Ye shall not eat of every tree of the garden? And the woman said unto the serpent, We may eat of the fruit of the trees of the garden: but of the fruit of the tree which is in the midst of the garden, God hath said, Ye shall not eat of it, neither shall ye touch it, lest ye die. And the serpent said unto the woman, Ye shall not surely die: for God doth know that in the day ye eat thereof, then your eyes shall be opened, and ye shall be as gods, knowing good and evil. And when the woman saw that the tree was good for food, and that it was pleasant to the eyes, and a tree to be desired to make one wise, she took of the fruit thereof, and did eat, and gave also unto her husband with her; and he did eat.

Genesis 3:1-6

It is amazing that she could say, "...God hath said...," yet succumb to what the devil said so very easily. Even today, people know what God has said, yet when they see things that dangle in front of them or when they feel they can gain wisdom from something, they are seduced.

Blessed is the man that endureth temptation: for when he is tried, he shall receive the crown of life, which the Lord hath promised to them that love Him. Let no man say when he is tempted, I am tempted of God: for God cannot be tempted with evil, neither tempteth He any man: but every man is tempted, when he is drawn away of his own lust, and enticed. Then when lust hath conceived, it bringeth forth sin: and sin, when it is finished, bringeth forth death.

James 1:12-15

We have already exposed the one who tempts us. But, let us look at Second Corinthians 11:3 for a reminder: "But I fear, lest by any means, as the serpent beguiled Eve through his subtlety, so your minds should be corrupted from the simplicity that is in Christ" (II Cor. 11:3). Notice that the Scripture speaks of "the simplicity that is in Christ."

"For this cause, when I could no longer forbear, I sent to know your faith, lest by some means the tempter have tempted you, and our labor be in vain" (I Thess. 3:5). We have labored over many in our church in vain. We have worked with people and given them many warnings, but they were "too smart" to hear the pastors. They thought they knew better than we did. Where are they today? Out of church and all messed up.

The Power of Temptation

The power of temptation is seen in Genesis 3:1-6 and Genesis 3:10-13. Let us now look at First Kings 11:1,4:

But King Solomon loved many strange women, together with the daughter of Pharaoh, women of the Moabites, Ammonites, Edomites, Zidonians, and Hittites... For it came to pass, when Solomon was old, that his wives turned away his heart after other gods....

Solomon had more wisdom than anyone on the face of the earth, but it did not seem to be enough. He wanted more. People do not succeed because they are smart; they succeed because they are spiritual. Those women turned Solomon's heart away from God to other gods, "...and his heart was not perfect with the Lord his God, as was the heart of David his father."

The Promise to the Tempted

Temptations will always be there, but God has given us a promise:

There hath no temptation taken you but such as is common to man: but God is faithful, who will not suffer you to be tempted above that ye are able; but will with the temptation also make a way to escape, that ye may be able to bear it.

I Corinthians 10:13

In every temptation, God has a "back door." It is unlocked, but the person who is being tempted must turn the knob and run. Some people have said, "Pastor, we had sex because we couldn't control it." It could have been controlled, if they had not gone as far with one another as they did. People cannot get into trouble if they are not in the room alone. They need to run out that "back door" of escape that God has provided or pay the price. No one should say he is tempted beyond his ability to control; there is a door. There is always a door, but sometimes people turn their backs to the door, face their lusts and enter therein. They cannot see the door because they are so attracted by their lusts.

"For in that He Himself hath suffered being tempted, He is able to succor them that are tempted" (Heb. 2:18) God is able to help those who are tempted. Jesus was tempted, so He knows what it is. What a promise! There is a door of escape, and we have a God who understands temptation.

Deliverance From Our Past Sinfulness

"...Old things are passed away; behold, all things are become new" (II Cor. 5:17). How does God deliver us from our past sinfulness? He makes all things new. God does not make rebuilt "carburetors." He makes new Christians. We are delivered from our past by something new.

God not only forgives us and pardons our past, but He also frees us from prison. How does that happen? If the old man is forgiven, a person becomes a new man. He is not an old man set free, he is a new man set free. We have new life.

Ephesians 4:22-32 shows us seven new things people receive as a result of new life in God:

A New Mind

The Book of Ephesians tells us that we have a new mind. "...And be renewed in the spirit of your mind..." (Eph. 4:23). We do not think like we used to. Most of us were captives of our minds, which were under the captivity of satan. Our thoughts were ugly, dirty and impure. But, the Bible says, "Unto the pure all things are pure..." (Titus 1:15). We have new minds.

A New Man

Ephesians 4:24 tells us we are a new man. "...that ye put on the new man, which after God is created in righteousness and true holiness." If a person is going to be a new man, it is time to act like and think like a new man. He should not only go for the "goodies" (blessings) from God; he should get a new life from Him.

A New Membership

Once a person becomes a Christian, he belongs to a different crowd. But, the devil has really had some of us fooled. Yes, we need to win our friends to the Lord, but there comes a time when we must refuse to be a part of our crowd of friends who refuse God.

People say, "You know, I've been friends with these people for years. Now, you're telling me not to be their friend?" Yes! People wonder why old friends and friendships are so binding and why those old friendships are so strong. It is because we are not as new as we think. We need to be renewed daily.

"Wherefore putting away lying, speak every man truth with his neighbor: for we are members one of another" (Eph. 4:25). We are members of the Body of Christ. This is a strength of a Christian's life. Some might say, "I don't like everyone in the church." But, why is it that they like the people in the world? The people of God are not perfect, but they are part of a body in which we also have membership.

Consider clay. It can be found in various places. There is primary clay and secondary clay. Secondary clay may be compared to someone who is considered to be a lesser person. However, it is easier to mold and shape secondary clay into the image the potter wants. Every type of clay has to go through a drying out period before it can be shaped into the image that the potter has designed. Once it is dried out, then it is watered. Its old substance has to be dried out, then the new substance, water (which for us is symbolic of the Holy Spirit), is poured on it.

The reason some of us have so much trouble with our new membership is that we have never "dried out." We are still part of that old world. One foot is in God, and one foot is in the world. We do whatever we want to do.

Some of us may not understand. People need to let all the "water" of the old man be dried out; then they can be shaped with the "water" put in by the Potter. Then they can also be fused and fired. People need to let the Word of God cleanse them and take out the impurities, so the new "purities" can be put into the "clay" to shape, make and mold it. We need to become part of a new membership.

A New Master

Some people have been slaves to King Heroin. It is amazing how heroin addicts will be subservient to a king who did not die for them. Heroin will kill them, and they serve it more faithfully than they serve Jesus who is the King of kings.

Ephesians 4:27 says, "...neither give place to the devil." Once a person is saved, the devil is no longer his master. Then the devil could tell a person to eat of the tree, but the person could tell the devil, "You are not my master. God said, 'No,' and He is my Master. I will not eat of the tree. It looks pleasant, and yes, it is enticing, but I will not do it, because I listen to a different voice now."

A New Method

"Let him that stole steal no more: but rather let him labor, working with his hands the thing which is good..." (Eph. 4:28). It is not a sin to work; it is a sin to be lazy. It is a sin to sit back and let everyone else do all the work. It is sin for a person to use the resources of welfare when he is strong enough to make it on his own.

Christians who do not want to get up and go to work in the morning are in trouble. The above verse of Scripture says that they should be working those things which are good. People should be working the things which are good so that they "…may have to give to him that needeth." This is the new method.

A New Ministry

In addition to the above-mentioned new things that God puts into people's lives when He delivers them from their past sinfulness, there is a new ministry. "Let no corrupt communication proceed out of your mouth, but that which is good to the use of edifying, that it may minister grace unto the hearers" (Eph. 4:29). Our new ministry is to edify and not to break down. It is to uplift and not to gossip. If one cannot bless another, it is better for him not to say anything.

A New Mercy

We need to be people of mercy. "And be ye kind one to another, tenderhearted, forgiving one another even as God for Christ's sake hath forgiven you" (Eph. 4:32).

Chapter Four

The Manifestation for the Poor

It should be stated that the Word of the Lord about the poor is being put into Love Gospel Assembly. God has been speaking to us about this so much. His Word is protecting the vision, which includes reaching the poor and reaching the cities. But, unfortunately, we have not yet understood the Word, because we have not taken the time to let it reverberate. However, it will reverberate, and we are going to see the vision happen.

If we look carefully, we will see. If we do not look carefully, we will not see. If Jesus had not looked over Jerusalem, He would not have wept. The reason He wept was He saw the condition of that city.

The Spirit of the Lord is upon Me because He hath anointed Me to preach the gospel to the poor; He hath sent Me to heal the brokenhearted, to preach deliverance to the captives, and recovering of sight to the blind....

Luke 4:18

We have discussed the message for the poor, the ministry for the poor and the miracles for the poor. Let us now turn our attention to the manifestation for the poor. Jesus promises recovery of sight to the poor, the outcast, those especially who were cast aside by the religious communities.

The urban communities seem to have rejected Jesus. But, they have not really rejected Jesus; the real Jesus has not been presented to them. An impotent, charlatan Jesus has been presented to them. They have not seen the real Jesus who cares, loves, heals broken hearts, delivers from captivity and opens the eyes of the blind.

How can we know this real Jesus? We do not know Jesus through intellect, academics, a system of theology, expert hermeneutics or exegesis of historical linguistic interpretations. We come to know the real Jesus the same way Peter knew Him.

When Jesus asked the disciples, "Whom do men say that I the Son of man am?" Peter said, "Thou art the Christ, the Son of the living God." Jesus said, "...flesh and blood hath not revealed it unto thee, but My Father which is in heaven" (Matt. 16:17). Peter knew Christ because he had a revelation. He knew Christ because by the Spirit of God he was able to see the real Jesus. Peter did not learn that in his fishing boat or sitting in a classroom or through a synagogue system of learning. He learned it from God. The Father opened Peter's eyes, enabling him to see Jesus.

The people of the world do not see Jesus, because they have no revelation of Jesus. Christians in general do not preach with revelation; when we do, it is not geared to those in an urban setting. People have heard, but they have not seen the vision. Jesus said He would restore sight to the blind. Some think the vision is something mystical or a set of lessons to be learned. No, it is not these things. To understand the vision, people need a revelation. However, restoration of sight will not make us great. Even Peter made a lot of mistakes after he had received revelation, and by the end of Matthew 16, Jesus said to Peter, "Get thee behind Me, satan."

The manifestation to the poor is given so that they might see. Remember, in Luke 4:18 Jesus quotes Isaiah 61. He speaks of "recovering of sight to the blind," but in Isaiah 61 it says, "...the opening of the prison to them that are bound...." It seems as though these are two different statements. How could Jesus, quoting Isaiah, come up with something totally different? In order to understand, we must dig deeper.

Considering the historical framework, we understand that prisons in Isaiah's time were dark dungeons. When men bound in dungeons were set free, they saw the light of day, and in that sense, their eyes were opened. In Hebrew, Isaiah 61 says,"the opening of the eye." It signifies the ability to see clearly, as contrasted with the gloomy atmosphere of prison. Consequently, when Jesus spoke of the "recovering of sight to the blind," it was not so different from what Isaiah had said. Jesus used different terms so the men in the synagogue, men of religious background, could understand Him.

In the prisons of today, there is something that is referred to as "a prison within a prison." Inmates call it the "hole." When prisoners go into the hole, it is much like it was in

Isaiah's day—dark and gloomy. There is no sign of life. No one enters, no one leaves. There is only one person in a small area of confinement. Then, when the person is released from the hole, he is able to see once again; the gloom is gone. This is what God is saying: He has come to the poor who live in "the gloom of prison."

There are people out in the streets who are in that sort of prison. The poor, oppressed and needy are in prison. Jesus said He had come to take away the gloom that obscures their sight. In fact, referring to the blind and the opening of the eyes, the original Greek has to do with "smoke." It is like a fog, and those who are in that condition cannot see clearly enough to walk without tripping. The poor cannot see Jesus clearly because of their cloud of poverty, oppression, poor nourishment and lack of spiritual knowledge.

Further investigating the original text, it is interesting to note that the English words *recovering* and *sight* are actually one word in Greek. Similarly, the phrase *opening of the prison* in Hebrew is basically one concept.

As we look at the Greek, English and Hebrew of these two scriptures, there are three words that can be used to describe what happens when there is that recovering of sight: there is *reversal, recovering* and *restoration.*

Reversal

In the reversal, God enables us to look back. Spiritually, we are able not only to look forward, but also to look back. It is like having eyes in the back of our head.

We are able to look back to the cross and see our salvation. When we lead someone to the Lord, we do not encourage them to look back at their own past, but to look back at the cross. Why do they need to look back at the cross? To see their salvation. Jesus will not only give sight to the poor, but He will also turn them around and point them toward the cross. Although they are poor, they can look back at the cross and be saved.

But, if our eyes are not opened in order to look back and see the cross, how can we see our salvation? How can we expect people to be saved when their "eyesight," their ability to look back at the cross, is clouded? How can people be saved if there is not a revelation of the cross?

How is the cross revealed? It is revealed when God opens our eyes. He takes us out of the darkness of dungeons so that we can look back and see the cross. The poor must be able to see the cross.

For this cause we also, since the day we heard it, do not cease to pray for you, and to desire that ye might be filled with the knowledge of His will in all wisdom and spiritual understanding; that ye might walk worthy of the Lord unto all pleasing, being fruitful in every good work, and increasing in the knowledge of God; strengthened with all might, according to His glorious power, unto all patience and longsuffering with joyfulness; giving thanks unto the Father, which hath made us meet to be partakers of the inheritance of the saints in light: who hath delivered us from the power of darkness, and hath translated us into the kingdom of His dear Son: in whom we have redemption through

His blood, even the forgiveness of sins: who is the image of the invisible God, the firstborn of every creature: for by Him were all things created, that are in heaven, and that are in earth, visible and invisible, whether they be thrones, or dominions, or principalities, or powers: all things were created by Him, and for Him: and He is before all things, and by Him all things consist. And He is the head of the body, the church: who is the beginning, the firstborn from the dead; that in all things He might have the preeminence. For it pleased the Father that in Him should all fulness dwell; and, having made peace through the blood of His cross, by Him to reconcile all things unto Himself; by Him, I say, whether they be things in earth, or things in heaven.

Colossians 1:9-20

Verse 13 says, "…who hath delivered us from the power of darkness…." Before people are saved, they are under the power of darkness. They cannot see the cross. They cannot see anything clearly, because they are in darkness.

Let us examine what Paul said to the Colossian church.

God's Power for Man's Lust

"…and, having made peace through the blood of His cross, by Him to reconcile all things unto Himself…" (Col. 1:20). The cross is the measure of God's power for man's lust. Without the cross, we will remain in our lustful condition.

"Therefore if any man be in Christ, he is a new creature: old things are passed away; behold, all things are become new" (II Cor. 5:17). It is the power of the cross that changes our state of living from lustfulness to abundant life in Him.

God's Passion for Man's Loneliness

The cross is also the manifestation of God's passion for man's loneliness. Through the cross God is saying He has power. Through it He is also saying He has passion. Jesus' death on the cross is a demonstration of God's love for sinners.

At the cross God showed passion for man's loneliness. When people are alone, and no one seems to care, they can turn around and see the cross. This is the place where they can see Jesus.

"God commendeth His love toward us, in that, while we were yet sinners, Christ died for us" (Rom. 5:8). The word *sinner* means one who is separated, having missed the mark. A sinner is one who is distant from God. We could say, "God commended His love toward us while we were away from Him, having missed the mark (not having attained). This was when Christ died for us."

While we were lonely, God commended His love toward us. Loneliness is not restricted by economic, racial or cultural barriers. Those who do not have God cannot say they are not lonely. Money cannot heal a heart. Lust and sex cannot satisfy a soul. All people are lonely until they come into union and oneness with God.

Drug abuse is prevalent in our society because lonely people are trying to fill the spiritual void in their lives. But, the only thing that can fill that void is the love of God. As God gives light, He takes away the darkness of the dungeon, and people are able to turn to the cross and see His love.

I started abusing wine and drugs at the age of 13; even at that early age I felt an emptiness. That emptiness stayed with me no matter how many bottles of muscatel I drank. I would go to sleep in a drunken stupor and still wake up empty. I would inject heroin into my body and still be empty. Eventually, my drug involvement led me into a life of crime, and I ended up in jail. I had been alone while I was on the streets, and I was alone while I was in jail. The loneliness did not go away until I accepted Jesus on a cold December day in 1962. That is when I began to understand and experience God's love. The dark scales were taken from my eyes, and I was able to turn around and see the cross that said Jesus had died for me.

When the Christians told me that Jesus loved me, I thought they were making a mistake. I am a Jew, and I thought Jesus was a Gentile and that Jesus only loved Gentiles. I had been raised around Gentile children who had never told me about Jesus' resurrection from the dead. Thus, I figured at least the God I believed in was still alive. I was in total blindness until, at the age of 27 my eyes were opened. Now, I understand the demonstration of God's passion for my loneliness at the cross.

God's Peace for Man Who Is Lost

"...and, having made peace through the blood of the cross..." (Col. 1:20). Where can a person find peace? It does not come from a liquor bottle or a hypodermic needle; peace cannot be found in snorting drugs. Peace comes from the blood that came down from the cross.

When a person is lost, he is not at peace. This is why some people go crazy. They are not only filled with lust and loneliness, but they are lost. They do not know where they are going. Despite education and accumulation of wealth, people who do not know God have no knowledge of where they are going. They may have made plans, but they are uncertain about the future.

A person who is at peace with God has no delusions of grandeur. He dreams the dreams of God. He dreams in God, with God and for God. The poor on the streets have no such dreams. They live hopeless lives. They have not seen the power, the passion and the peace of God on the cross.

God's Pardon for Man's Lack

When we look at the cross, we also see God's pardon (forgiveness). Because Jesus died in our place, we are set free. God has pardoned us. "For He hath made Him to be sin for us, who knew no sin; that we might be made the righteousness of God in Him" (II Cor. 5:21).

Why is the cross the method of God's pardon for man's lack? Simply because man does not have the ability to cover up his own sin, nor does man have the ability to cause another man's sins to be forgiven. Man falls short when it comes to spiritual pardon. A governor can loose a person from prison, but only God can set people free from sin.

Throughout history men have tried to cover their own sins. The first man who tried did not succeed. When Adam and Eve sinned, they realized they were naked and used fig leaves to try to cover their nakedness. But, when God came, they hid. Intuitively and instinctively, they knew the covering they had made for themselves was not enough to cover them in front of God.

People can put on nice clothes and fool the masses, but God sees through clothes. There is only one thing that blocks God's sight. It is the blood of Jesus. When God sees the blood, He looks no further. God is able to pardon us because of the blood that was shed at the cross.

Recovery

Recovery is not looking back, it is being loved back. It is being brought back to the place where we originally were intended to be. Man was not created to be separated from God, but to walk with God. Unfortunately, man has separated himself from God by sinning. Once we have our eyes opened, we can see God's will for His creation.

Sinners need to hear this, but Christians need to hear it as well. Once God has opened our eyes so that we might be loved back, we are not to live unto ourselves, but we are to be one with God. We are not to be absorbed with our ideas, ideals or ideologies, but we are to be one with God. This is the conflict most Christians have.

People want to be Christians, but they want to know what is the minimum they can give to God and remain saved. They want to know how much they can get away with. This attitude is prevalent in the Church.

Our desires and personal achievements in life are very important. God wants us to achieve. He wants us to attain to great places in Him. But, there is a difference in wanting to achieve a great place for ourselves and wanting to achieve a great place in Him.

Some of us were loved back to God when we were saved. God turned us around with His love, and He walked us back into fellowship with Him. However, some have turned around again and are slowly walking away from God. They stand in the middle; one hand is reaching for the things of God, the other hand is reaching for personal ambition. This is not why God has loved us, we were loved back so we could see our Savior. "...I have loved thee with an everlasting love; therefore with lovingkindness have I drawn thee" (Jer. 31:3).

If people are not loved back to and by Jesus, when they look at Jesus, they see a man. This is why there are so many different opinions and theologies today. There are many who have never been loved back to God. They are still walking in darkness. Christ can only be understood by those whose eyes have been opened.

The world can understand Christ as a man. Perhaps they even can understand Him to be a compassionate man. Nevertheless, the most they can understand about Jesus without their eyes being opened is that he was some kind of prophet.

People who are blind cannot see a complete revelation of the Person of Christ. Jesus reveals Himself to us by opening our eyes, then we are loved back into His presence. Let us examine several aspects of the Jesus to whom God causes us to be loved back.

He Is Love

Jesus is not merely loving, but He is love. In Romans 8:35 Paul asks, "Who shall separate us from the love of Christ?" Second Corinthians 5:14 states, "For the love of Christ constraineth us...." In John 15:13 we read, "Greater love hath no man than this, that a man lay down his life for his friends." What love! Jesus laid down His life out of love. This is the love that leads us back.

He Is Liberty

Jesus is the One who sets us free. He breaks the chains that keep people bound. No one else is going to do it. Jesus alone can do it. Galatians 5:1 says, "Stand fast therefore in the liberty wherewith Christ hath made us free...."

He Is Light

Without Jesus, we cannot see. Not only is Jesus the light giver, but He is the Light. Psalm 27:1 says, "The Lord is my light and my salvation...." Isaiah 60:20 says, "...for the Lord shall be thine everlasting light...." Micah 7:8 says, "...when I sit in darkness, the Lord shall be a light unto me." In John 8:12, Jesus states, "...I am the light of the world...."

He Is Loyal

Jesus is loyal. Many women have experienced the disloyalty of men, and the damage that has been done is incredible. In some instances this disloyalty has interrupted their relationship with God. They do not feel they can trust men, and now they are afraid to trust God. But, God is not a man. He is a Spirit. He can be trusted. He never leaves nor forsakes us. In Hebrews 13:5, Jesus states, "...I will never leave thee, nor forsake thee."

The psalmist understood God's loyalty; he said, "When my father and my mother forsake me, then the Lord will take me up" (Ps. 27:10). People should feel that way when their husband, wife, boyfriend or girlfriend forsakes them.

They should feel that way when their best friend does not want to talk to them anymore. They should feel that way when the pastor does not preach what they want to hear. People should feel that way when the elders do not bend over backward for them. God will never forsake them. The Bible says, "...yet have I not seen the righteous forsaken, nor his seed begging bread" (Ps. 37:25). God is always there. He is loyal.

He Is Life

In John 11:25, Jesus said, "...I am the resurrection, and the life...." John 10:10 says, "...I am come that they might have life, and that they might have it more abundantly." In order to know what life is, we have to see Jesus. Once we see Jesus as Savior, we are going to have life. Without Jesus, those in the world are merely existing, but in Christ people have life.

He Is Lasting

A certain lady who had tried drugs wanted to know if the things of Jesus would last. She said she had tried marijuana and enjoyed it, but it did not last. She had tried alcohol and liked it, but it did not last. She had tried men and enjoyed them, but it did not last. She wanted to know if her experience with Jesus would be just another short journey. She wanted to know if there was something else that she had to find after an encounter with Jesus.

The thrill of substances, material possessions and money fades. As soon as a person gets used to having one thing, he wants something else. Jesus is not a substance that loses its appeal. He is the Savior who lives forever. "And even to your old age I am He; even to hoar hairs will I carry you: I have made, and I will bear; even I will carry, and will deliver you" (Isa. 46:4).

Will this last? Yes, it will last. Will it stay as good as it is in the beginning? That's up to the individual. If one loses his first love, it will not get better. If after being saved, money, ambitions or goals become a person's first love, it will not get better. But, if a person continues in a committed Christian walk, it gets better and better.

He Is Lord

One of the greatest problems in Christianity is that people have allowed Jesus to be their Savior, but they have not allowed Him to be their Lord. Jesus is to be both Savior and Lord. *Savior* means He is a deliverer. He sets us free. That's what salvation means. *Lord* means He is Master.

Restoration

In the reversal, we look back to see the cross. In the recovery, we are loved back, and we see Christ. When we are restored, we are led back so that we might see the Church. It is essential that we see the importance of the Church, not a specific church, but a coming into the Church, the Body of Christ, and functioning in a local body.

We look back to the cross to see our salvation, and we are loved back to Christ to see our Savior. Similarly, we must look back to the Church to see our sainthood. If we do not see the Church, we cannot see that in Christ we are saints.

There exists a theology about sainthood which is quite questionable. This teaching maintains that one must be dead in order to be a saint. The New Testament does not tell us anything about death being prerequisite to sainthood. Let us examine a few Scriptures which deal with this issue.

Romans 1:7 states, "To all that be in Rome, beloved of God, called to be saints...." This verse actually says, "...called saints...." The words *to be* are italicized in the King James Version, meaning they do not appear in the original. According to the apostle Paul, Christians are called saints. Consequently, we are to act like saints.

First Corinthians 1:2 is another verse of Scripture referring to Christians as saints. Paul writes, "Unto the church of God which is at Corinth, to them that are sanctified in Christ Jesus, called to be saints...." Anyone who knows anything about Corinth knows that these people were not a group likely to be called saints, yet Paul called them saints. If they were saints, Christians of today are saints also.

Following are more verses of Scripture that deal with sainthood: "Paul, an apostle of Jesus Christ by the will of God, to the saints which are at Ephesus, and to the faithful in Christ..." (Eph. 1:1). "Paul and Timotheus, the servants of Jesus Christ, to all the saints in Christ Jesus which are at Philippi, with the bishops and deacons..." (Phil. 1:1). "Paul, an apostle of Jesus Christ by the will of God, and Timotheus our brother, to the saints and faithful brethren in Christ which are at Colosse..." (Col. 1:1-2).

The word *saint* in all of these verses comes from the same Greek word. It means "sacred; clean; innocent; modest; chaste; perfect." This is the same word that was used to describe the Corinthian church. It also means "blameless." In Christ God has taken away all the wrong that we have done. We are blameless.

The basic meaning of the word *saint* is "to be set apart." Jesus has caused us to be blameless, now we are set apart for God's purposes. Let us look at some of these.

Set Apart to Worship

Many people do not think worship is important, but if they are not worshipers, their experience with God is incomplete. We have been set apart to worship God. If we do not worship God, who will? Can the heathen worship God? Jesus said that if we do not worship Him, the rocks would cry out, not the heathen. We must worship.

In His conversation with the woman at the well, Jesus said, "God is a Spirit: and they that worship Him must worship Him in spirit and in truth" (John 4:24). We need to learn how to worship in spirit and in truth. We cannot worship in theology.

Set Apart for Witness

But ye shall receive power, after that the Holy Ghost is come upon you: and ye shall be witnesses unto Me both in Jerusalem, and in all Judea, and in Samaria, and unto the uttermost part of the earth.

Acts 1:8

Who is going to witness for Jesus? Some people think it's going to be the President of the United States. We look for the congressmen, mayors, judges and community leaders to do it. Yet, Jesus said that the Church would receive His power and be His witnesses.

Set Apart for Warfare

Anyone who comes to Christ in order to breeze through life does not know what Christianity is all about. Christianity is a life of warfare. Paul commanded Timothy to war a good warfare. "This charge I commit unto thee, son Timothy, according to the prophecies which went before on thee, that thou by them mightest war a good warfare" (I Tim. 1:18). We are set apart by God to war with the devil, not to be afraid of the devil and run. The only time we are to flee is when sin tempts us. Other than that, we are to confront the devil and overcome him.

Some Christians are afraid to dedicate more of themselves to God. They think the closer they get to God, the more the devil will bother them. Some feel relatively safe when the devil is not bothering them; they feel that is a nice way to live, and they would like for things to remain that way. They may be comfortable with that, but it is not what God wants. He wants us to be set apart for warfare.

Set Apart to Walk

"Walking" in the Bible has to do with God's purity. "This I say then, Walk in the Spirit, and ye shall not fulfill the lust of the flesh" (Gal. 5:16). The Bible also says to walk in love, walk in light, walk circumspectly and walk carefully. The Word of God constantly speaks about our walk as one of holiness and closeness to Him.

Set Apart to the Word

We are set apart to be students of the Word of God. When a person does not know God's Word, he cannot know God's will. "Thy Word is a lamp unto my feet, and a light unto my path" (Ps. 119:105).

It is amazing to see how easily Christians claim that they know God and know all about what He wants. Many new

Christians express their views about how God moves and what He does; they have just come to the Lord, yet they feel they are thoroughly knowledgeable about the ways of God. Others have been faithfully serving God for decades and still do not fully understand God. Just when they think they know how He works, God does it a different way. In order to understand how God works, it is imperative that we set ourselves apart to study the Word of God.

Set Apart to Work

God is not the author of laziness. If someone is lazy, he did not get it from God. Some people do not understand what it means to work hard. Others think if there is not the punching of a clock or doing some heavy manual labor, a person is not working. There are people who think that because a person sits behind a desk, no work is done. But, there are all kinds of work. Some jobs require much physical activity, whereas other jobs require much emotional and mental activity.

It is not necessarily what type of work a person does that is most important, but that he does a good job at what he is assigned. "Therefore, My beloved brethren, be ye steadfast, unmovable, always abounding in the work of the Lord, forasmuch as ye know that your labor is not in vain in the Lord" (I Cor. 15:58). "Let him that stole steal no more: but rather let him labor, working with his hands the thing which is good, that he may have to give to him that needeth" (Eph. 4:28).

Chapter Five

The Mercy for the Poor

The mercy for the poor is to set at liberty those who are oppressed. The King James Version of Luke 4:18 says, "...to set at liberty them that are bruised...." It really means those who are oppressed. Jesus came to set at liberty the oppressed.

The rich are not an oppressed people. The poor are oppressed. Although rich people are the oppressors of the poor, not all rich people are oppressors. One should be very slow to judge. It all depends on how a person became rich. Oppression comes from a person's desire to get rich; in many instances, people step on others in order to achieve that goal.

Over the years we have left the message of the oppressed to the liberal theologians and the liberal Christians. But, the fact of the matter is the Bible is filled with references to oppression and oppressors.

There are those who preach about prosperity. God prospers people. But, the gospel is not merely a gospel of prosperity. The Bible speaks more about oppression than it does about prosperity. People find it easier to speak about prosperity because with it comes blessing. It is more difficult to deal with oppression because with it comes burden. People do not want to be burdened, because they do not understand the Word of God.

The poor who have not received Christ who are oppressed are sinners even as the rich who have not received Christ are sinners. They are alienated and separated from God because they have not received Jesus as Lord and Savior. Even though rich and poor are in the same spiritual condition, there is a big difference. The unsaved poor are sinners, but on top of that, they are sinned against. There are rich people who are sinners, and they sin against the poor simply because they are poor. The poor are oppressed by those who use them to elevate themselves to higher levels of power and riches. Thus, in dealing with the poor, one is dealing not only with people who are sinners needing salvation, but with people who are downtrodden because they have been sinned against.

The poor are confused because they are preached to about their sins, while the rich are not preached to about their sins against the poor. The urban poor feel that God is the God of those who oppress them. In their eyes God seems to be smiling upon the rich. In their state of oppression, the urban poor feel that God is not concerned about them.

Poor people hear those who have been monetarily and materially blessed say the reason God has blessed them is that He loves them. They point to their new cars, clothes and shoes as proof. Therefore, the ones who are without these things feel that God does not love them or He would have blessed them in the same way.

The Church is not telling the poor about the love of Jesus Christ who came and died for them. Nor is the Church telling them that Christ does not care about how they look, rather He looks beyond the outer man and sees the hurt within. Although the human eye cannot see it, God has seen their hurt and pain. However, the Church's refusal to deal with urban issues gives the impression that God has refused to deal with the city and city people. When the people of oppressed, poverty-stricken communities see churches leaving, churches not caring, churches with doors closed to them, churches that will not feed them or clothe them, churches that do not extend themselves toward them, they think that God has left. The Christians' departure from urban areas has left the impression that God has gone uptown to live with the oppressors.

The poor then assume that if God and His church people do not care, why should they care? Thus, it makes no difference to them if they shoot somebody in the head. The poor do not have a biblical concept of life. It has not been taught to them.

When the Church turned its back on the poor, it was as though the poor saw the back of God. When the poor saw the mass exodus of Christians, it seemed as though they saw an exodus of God from that area. The biblical exodus was an exodus from oppression, not God exiting from the oppressed.

Our concepts are backward, and we must straighten them out. Is God the God of the oppressor or is He the God of the oppressed?

When the oppressed cast out their oppressors by military or other means, they become the oppressors. All so-called oppressors were once oppressed, but they forgot about it when they came into the lap of luxury. Likewise, many Christians have forgotten who they were before Jesus saved them.

Often people are assumed to be moral if they wear three-piece suits. We assume morality because people are clean-shaven and doing well financially. Conversely, some assume all poor people are immoral. However, morality is not based on economic, educational or ethnic status. People with reason and intellect are not necessarily moral. A man with reason and absence of morality, could be the worst criminal, because immorality is not expected of him. We tend to trust presidents of corporations and people with Harvard or Yale degrees, but we need to be careful.

We need to take a serious look at the people who have been oppressed, those with whom Jesus was concerned. In order to do that, we will look at eight Hebrew words that speak of oppression, oppressors or the oppressed.

1. *Nagas* means "to oppress; exploit; force; or exert pressure." Thus, we understand that the oppressor exerts pressure on the oppressed. The devil is an oppressor; he exerts pressure. God leads, the devil pushes.

   When a person needs to do something quickly, even if it seems godly and righteous, it is rarely done properly. Undue pressure does not come from God.

In the English translations of the Book of Exodus the oppressor is considered to be a "taskmaster." A taskmaster exerts pressure to get the work done. *Nagas* not only pertains to a taskmaster, but it also pertains to a "slave driver." In the Semitic language the root meaning of *nagas* is thought to be "overwhelmed with work." "And the taskmasters hasted them, saying, Fulfil your works and your daily tasks..." (Exod. 5:13). The taskmasters forcefully drove the slaves to do work. This is oppression.

People were pressured not only by tasks, they also were pressured by taxes. In biblical times a tax collector took as much money from the people as he wanted to take. Even though the tax collectors in those times were most hated, Jesus came to save them also. He went into their homes, ate with them, saved them, lifted them up and changed them from oppressors to liberators.

When someone is forced into labor or has to pay outlandish taxes, he is oppressed in the worst way. When a person is taxed to such an extent that he is not able to eat, or when a person is forcibly made to work and there is no remuneration, it is oppressive. There is nothing more oppressive than slavery. Seldom does a rich person live under that kind of oppression.

2. *Anah* is the second Hebrew word we will consider. *Anah* relates to the type of oppression that degrades

the poor. It is easy for people to oppress the poor, because they do not have the money or the power to stand against oppression.

Anah means "to oppress, exploit, humiliate, degrade, subdue or subject, dominate, afflict, force or violate."

When *anah* speaks of violation, it refers to women. Women have no concept of the concern God has for the violations they have endured. They have been taken advantage of and violated by men, abused and stepped on. In many instances, because of their poverty and terrible life circumstances, some women have not been able to circumvent abusive treatment. But, God has saved them, and hopefully, these women have been able to let God bring them out of the state in which they found themselves because of the oppression.

Generally, it is not women who oppress women. It is usually men who oppress women. But, Jesus has come to set women free from that oppression. They need never let men oppress them again. They are set free! They do not have to be violated anymore. They do not have to be talked down to or pushed aside anymore. Jesus is on their side.

Even though Jesus is on the side of violated women, they are never going to overcome their oppression until they overcome their attitude toward men because of their oppression. If women harbor negative attitudes toward men because of oppression, they are not truly set free; they are still oppressed. As long as women have an overall negative attitude toward men, they will not be able to fully follow God. If a woman mistrusts her father, she will have a hard time trusting God. Unfortunately, many men who have oppressed women are their fathers.

These men, these fathers, have violated the women, and they have violated their mothers in their presence. They have violated their brothers and sisters. They have violated the whole neighborhood. Women who have been violated have a very bad concept of men. The only thing that will completely set them free from that oppression is a cleansing of the heart, which only God can do.

The reason the word *Anah* is especially relative to women is that one of its meanings is "forcing a person to submit." Oppression is not something that just happens. There are agents that cause it to happen.

And she answered him, Nay, my brother, do not force me; for no such thing ought to be done in Israel: do not thou this folly... Howbeit he would not hearken unto her voice: but, being stronger than she, forced her, and lay with her.

II Samuel 13:12,14

This is oppression! Rape is oppression. It is not merely a psychological problem, it is a sin that God despises.

In thee are men that carry tales to shed blood: and in thee they eat upon the mountains: in the midst of

*thee they commit lewdness. In thee have they dis-
covered their fathers' nakedness: in thee have they
humbled her that was set apart for pollution. And
one hath committed abomination with his neigh-
bour's wife; and another hath lewdly defiled his
daughter in law; and another in thee hath humbled
his sister, his father's daughter.*

Ezekiel 22:9-11

This was oppression. The oppressed never voluntar-
ily humble themselves to the oppressor. The oppressor actively oppresses, exploits and humiliates, yet
the oppressor rarely humbles himself before God.

3. *Lahats* speaks of oppression that causes a people to
   cry out for liberation. This word means "to be oppressed, to press, harass or drive back or corral." This
   kind of "hemming in" is similar to horses or cattle being driven into a corral where they cannot get out.

Since oppression is obviously a situation that is neither acceptable nor tolerable, a moment comes
when the weight of this oppression provokes unre-
strained tears, cries of pain and a call for a quick
liberation. There is an oppression that is so heavy
and powerful that it forces the oppressed to respond
with cries of agony.

There is a pattern here. First, there is oppression, then
there is the outcry of the oppressed. After that there is
an answering of the cry by the Omnipotent One, followed by the liberation, which is God coming into the
lives of the oppressed and setting them free.

Throughout the Bible one finds that every time oppressed people cried, God heard them. It is not worthless to cry. People should cry out to God when they are oppressed. He will set them free.

And thou shalt speak and say before the Lord thy God, A Syrian ready to perish was my father, and he went down into Egypt, and sojourned there with a few, and became there a nation, great, mighty, and populous: and the Egyptians evil entreated us, and afflicted us, and laid upon us hard bondage: and when we cried unto the Lord God of our fathers, the Lord heard our voice, and looked on our affliction, and our labor, and our oppression: and the Lord brought us forth out of Egypt with a mighty hand, and with an outstretched arm, and with great terribleness, and with signs, and with wonders: and He hath brought us into this place, and hath given us this land, even a land that floweth with milk and honey. And now, behold, I have brought the firstfruits of the land, which Thou, O Lord, hast given me. And thou shalt set it before the Lord thy God, and worship before the Lord thy God....

Deuteronomy 26:5-10

When God took the Israelites out of Egypt, He had heard their cry and delivered them. This called for a response from the people. Their response was a promise that when they harvested their firstfruits, they would worship the Lord. For many, this is the point at which deliverance from oppression fails. God releases people, but they do not understand that they owe Him worship and thanksgiving. We take God's power for granted.

4. *Osheq* implies that the rich rob from the poor. *Osheq* is a verb which means "to oppress, to obtain by violence and extortion." Economic exploitation and unjust sentences enforced by violent means are forms of injustice.

The oppressed suffer in their body and in their inner man. Oppression diminishes a person's self-esteem and causes his body to deteriorate. Restoration of dignity fights against oppression. Low self-esteem needs to be dealt with so people will grasp the understanding that we all are equal in God's sight. There is no one who is better than we, nor are we better than anyone else.

God can build our self-esteem. Women who have been violated need to understand this. They have no self-esteem because of the violation they have suffered. But, if someone lacks self-esteem, God says they can obtain it. Women who have been wronged by men do not have to walk around for the rest of their lives with their head down. God wants to lift their head.

Jesus has come into our lives, and He has cleansed us with His blood. Thus, we are clean and pure, and we should think highly of ourselves, because the Greater One lives in us. "...greater is He that is in you, than he that is in the world" (I John 4:4).

5. *Tok* speaks of oppression that employs lies. The thought of an oppressor telling the truth is ridiculous. The devil is a liar and the father of lies. Because the oppressor lies, his father is the devil.

The word *Tok* is seldom used in the Old Testament (four times). It means "oppression and tyranny." It speaks strongly of deception—lies and fraud. "Wickedness is in the midst thereof: deceit and guile depart not from her streets" (Ps. 55:11). This is an accurate description of city neighborhoods.

If people are not careful, those who are oppressed will oppress them by lying, stealing, deceiving or taking peoples' money. If someone were to take *their* money, they would kill that person; but they feel it is okay to take other people's money. Unfortunately, in addition to oppressing other people, oppressed people oppress each other.

6. *Dak* acknowledges that oppression exists, but also implies that there is hope. *Dak* is derived from the verb *dakah* which means "to wear out by rubbing." When a person is oppressed, he is being worn out, worn to a frazzle.

This verb is rare. It usually is translated as "oppressed, troubled or downtrodden," and it appears only six times, chiefly in the Psalms.

O let not the oppressed return ashamed: let the poor and needy praise Thy name.

Psalm 74:21

The Lord also will be a refuge for the oppressed, a refuge in times of trouble.

Psalm 9:9

Arise, O Lord; O God, lift up Thine hand: forget not the humble.

Psalm 10:12

In these Scriptures God is revealed as the One who makes possible the hope of a new order of things. Oppression may be real, but even in that oppression there is hope, as long as there is a God. When people are oppressed, but they know God, the oppression does not have to be the end for them. They do not have to buckle under the oppression. They can have hope in God and call on Him.

7. *Yanah* indicates that the oppressor enslaves and kills the oppressed. This word occurs in the Bible approximately 20 times, mostly in Ezekiel. It means "to oppress, exploit, dominate in a brutal way, suppress and put an end to and despoil." It also means "to take everything away, to deceive, to cheat." The literal meaning suggests enslavement. The chief motive for this type of oppression is as far-reaching as murder.

"Behold, the princes of Israel, every one were in thee to their power to shed blood" (Ezek. 22:6). The people were in Israel to shed blood. A close study of Ezekiel 22 helps us to see this oppression by the prophets, priests, politicians and people. It is interesting to note that the people were oppressors. They had once been the oppressed, but when they got the land, they did not give equal opportunity to the strangers who came to their land.

Ezekiel defines the righteous person as one who does not oppress, but restores the debtor his pledge, commits no robbery, gives his bread to the hungry and covers the naked with his garment.

8. *Ratsats* implies that the poor are ground down so that they may be robbed. This verb literally means "to mash, to grind and to crush."

Job speaks of an individual who had seized something: "Because he hath oppressed and hath forsaken the poor; because he hath violently taken away an house which he builded not..." (Job 20:19). This person did not build the house, but took it away from someone. This is oppression.

Righteousness requires that we undo yokes and free those who are bound by them.

Is not this the fast that I have chosen? to loose the bands of wickedness, to undo the heavy burdens, and to let the oppressed go free, and that ye break every yoke? Is it not to deal thy bread to the hungry, and that thou bring the poor that are cast out to thy house? When thou seest the naked, that thou cover him; and that thou hide not thyself from thine own flesh?

Isaiah 58:6-7

People say they are good: they are saved, and they are not committing adultery or taking drugs. But, if they are not caring for the poor, they are not righteous. The Bible says that undoing the heavy burdens and letting the oppressed go free is righteousness.

Isaiah 53 speaks of Jesus dying on the cross. It tells how He suffered and healed us by His stripes. This Scripture has been quoted by preachers many times. In verse 7 of the same chapter is something equally important. It says, "He was oppressed." Women need to know that Jesus was oppressed. Thus, He is able to identify with the oppression some women have faced.

The Word of God is the historical agent of liberation. The oppressed determined that they would no longer yield to the oppressor because they were fully convinced that God gives freedom. Does this mean that people should sit back and say, "We know God can set us free from oppression"? No, that's not enough. God can set people free, but they have to be determined that they will no longer yield to the oppressor and that they will call on God. In calling on God, people are totally, unequivocally convinced that God can set them free. Their freedom is connected to an experience with God. Thus, their struggle turns into a profession of faith, rather than a military engagement.

Today we see oppressors around the world. Armies are raised up to fight military oppressors, but this is not the solution. When these armies win, they become the oppressors. Then, perhaps, another army will come in and oust the army that just won. On and on it goes.

In countries where the people are oppressed there is a constant changing of leadership. A group who complain about the oppression will take over and become the new oppressors. But, being oppressed does not give people the right to become oppressors. In fact, those who have been oppressed should be least likely to oppress. Christians should not disassociate themselves, but must be engaged in the struggle along with God, who was oppressed for us.

There are four groups of people who are most oppressed. These are the widows, the orphans, the poor and the prophets who speak against oppression. Throughout the Bible, oppression came against the prophets who spoke out against oppressions.

And it came to pass in process of time, that the king of Egypt died: and the children of Israel sighed by reason of the bondage, and they cried, and their cry came up unto God by reason of the bondage. And God heard their groaning, and God remembered His covenant with Abraham, with Isaac, and with Jacob. And God looked upon the children of Israel, and God had respect unto them.

Exodus 2:23-25

The Israelites were oppressed, and they cried. God heard their cry and brought their liberation. How did God bring liberation? In Exodus chapter 3, God went on a "hunting expedition." God went into the wilderness and searched out a man named Moses, whom He had supernaturally protected from death.

Moses had been brought up in the house of Pharaoh, although he had a Jewish heritage. Moses realized he was a Hebrew, and he said he was ready and willing to suffer with his people, to be in slavery with them, rather than enjoy the pleasures of sin, which only last for a season.

God met Moses in a lowly bush, because Moses was to go to a lowly, oppressed people. God revealed Himself to Moses in that burning bush that would not be consumed. From that bush God spoke to Moses and told him to go and set His people free.

And the angel of the Lord appeared unto him in a flame of fire out of the midst of a bush: and he looked, and, behold, the bush burned with fire, and the bush was not consumed. And Moses said, I will now turn aside, and see this great sight, why the bush is not burnt. And when the Lord saw that he turned aside to see, God called unto him out of the midst of the bush, and said, Moses, Moses. And he said, Here am I. And He said, Draw not nigh hither: put off thy shoes from off thy feet, for the place whereon thou standest is holy ground. Moreover He said, I am the God of thy father, the God of Abraham, the God of Isaac, and the God of Jacob. And Moses hid his face; for he was afraid to look upon God.

And the Lord said, I have surely seen the affliction of My people which are in Egypt, and have heard their cry by reason of their taskmasters; for I know their sorrows; and I am come down to deliver them out of the hand of the Egyptians, and to bring them up out of that land unto a good land and a large, unto a land flowing with milk and honey; unto the place of the Canaanites, and the Hittites, and the Amorites, and the Perizzites, and the Hivites, and the Jebusites. Now therefore, behold, the cry of the children of Israel is come unto Me: and I have also seen the oppression wherewith the Egyptians oppress them. Come now therefore, and I will send thee unto Pharaoh, that thou mayest bring forth My people the children of Israel out of Egypt.

Exodus 3:2-10

God is saying the same thing to the Body of Christ today. He has heard the cry of the ghettos. He has heard the cry from the crack houses. He has heard the cry from the empty buildings where men and women sleep. He has heard the cry of the homeless who are refusing the shelters, choosing to live on the streets because the shelters are so bad. God has heard their cry. He has come down to deliver them. It is time for us to arise and go to Pharaoh's house and say, "Let God's people go."

And Moses said unto God, Who am I, that I should go unto Pharaoh, and that I should bring forth the children of Israel out of Egypt? And He said, Certainly I will be with thee; and this shall be a token unto thee, that I have sent thee: When thou hast brought forth the people out of Egypt, ye shall serve God upon this mountain.

Exodus 3:11-12

The people of God may not feel equipped to do the things that God tells them to do, but certainly He will be with them. They need to be willing. God's people need to be willing to stand up and speak.

It is not important to keep the status quo, to be accepted by the evangelical, fundamental, pentecostal and charismatic churches of this country. The most important thing should not be to be seen with popular people. God's people need to walk in the streets among the oppressed and know that the presence of God in their lives can do those people some good.

Many of God's people will not have a television documentary written about them. The world at large will never know they existed. Many will never become famous, but if they do God's will, they will have achieved their life's purpose.

The oppressed need to know that there is a God who cares, there is a God who can set the oppressed free without military weaponry, there is a God who hears the cry of the oppressed.

Chapter Six

The God of the Oppressed

In the previous chapter we dealt with the oppressed. Now, we will consider the God of the oppressed. We do not see God projected as the God of the oppressed in our society. We do not teach this.

All of us have been challenged by the oppression of the poor, but even more, we need to be changed. The Word of the Lord must change us. If it merely stops at Challenge Street and never gets to Change Boulevard, we are in a lot of trouble. Let us consider what the Word of God has to say about the God of the oppressed.

Now there arose up a new king over Egypt, which knew not Joseph. And he said unto his people, Behold, the people of the children of Israel are more and mightier than we: come on, let us deal wisely with them; lest they multiply, and it come to pass, that, when there falleth out any war, they join also unto our enemies, and fight against us, and so get them up out of the land. Therefore they did set over

*them taskmasters to afflict them with their burdens.
And they built for Pharaoh treasure cities, Pithom
and Raamses. But the more they afflicted them, the
more they multiplied and grew. And they were
grieved because of the children of Israel. And the
Egyptians made the children of Israel to serve with
rigor: and they made their lives bitter with hard
bondage, in morter, and in brick, and in all manner
of service in the field: all their service, wherein they
made them serve, was with rigor.*

Exodus 1:8-14

*And it came to pass in process of time, that the king
of Egypt died: and the children of Israel sighed by
reason of the bondage, and they cried, and their cry
came up unto God by reason of the bondage. And
God heard their groaning, and God remembered His
covenant with Abraham, with Isaac, and with Jacob.
And God looked upon the children of Israel, and God
had respect unto them.*

*Now Moses kept the flock of Jethro his father in law,
the priest of Midian: and he led the flock to the backside of the desert, and came to the mountain of God,
even to Horeb. And the angel of the Lord appeared
unto him in a flame of fire out of the midst of a bush:
and he looked and, behold, the bush burned with fire,
and the bush was not consumed. And Moses said, I
will now turn aside, and see this great sight, why the
bush is not burnt. And when the Lord saw that he
turned aside to see, God called unto him out of the
midst of the bush, and said, Moses, Moses. And he*

said, Here am I. And He said, Draw not nigh hither: put off thy shoes from off thy feet, for the place whereon thou standest is holy ground. Moreover He said, I am the God of thy father, the God of Abraham, the God of Isaac, and the God of Jacob. And Moses hid his face; for he was afraid to look upon God.

And the Lord said, I have surely seen the affliction of my people which are in Egypt, and have heard their cry by reason of their taskmasters; for I know their sorrows....

Exodus 2:23-3:1-7

What a God! Sometimes we in the Church assume that God does not know what the oppressed are feeling in their bondage, but God knows.

And I am come down to deliver them out of the hand of the Egyptians, and to bring them up out of that land unto a good land and a large, unto a land flowing with milk and honey; unto the place of the Canaanites, and the Hittites, and the Amorites, and the Perizzites, and the Hivites, and the Jebusites. Now therefore, behold, the cry of the children of Israel is come unto Me: and I have also seen the oppression wherewith the Egyptians oppress them.

Exodus 3:8-9

Whether we intend to do so or not, in general the Body of Christ in this country portrays God as the God of the opulent, the rich. But, God is the God of the oppressed.

Remember, the poor who have not received Christ as Savior and Lord are not only sinners, but they also are sinned against. They believe that God is not concerned about them because they see the condition of those who sin against them. However, God is not the God of the opulent; He is not the God of the oppressor. God is the God of the poor and the oppressed. The Bible speaks of it so often that it is hard to understand why so few have seen it.

Why have only the black preachers seen this? God has given the Church a voice—why has it not cried out with those who have been oppressed and with those who have come out of oppression? The Church must change.

We need to look at God's relationship with the oppressed. To do this, we are going to consider three aspects of this relationship: First, we will consider the passion with which God sees. God sees with love. If God did not see with love, there would be no one saved. Secondly, we will consider the person whom God selects. Once God decides that the time for oppression is past, He selects a man and sends that man on a mission to set the oppressed free. Thirdly, we will consider the purpose for which God saves. He does not merely save individuals out of oppression so they will not be oppressed, but God has a purpose beyond their freedom from oppression.

The Passion With Which God Sees

And it came to pass in process of time, that the king of Egypt died: and the children of Israel sighed by reason of the bondage, and they cried, and their cry came up unto God by reason of the bondage. And God heard their groaning, and God remembered His covenant with Abraham, with Isaac, and with Jacob.

And God looked upon the children of Israel, and God had respect unto them.

Exodus 2:23-25

And the Lord said, I have surely seen the affliction of My people which are in Egypt, and have heard their cry by reason of their taskmasters; for I know their sorrows; and I am come down to deliver them out of the hand of the Egyptians, and to bring them up out of that land unto a good land and a large, unto a land flowing with milk and honey....

Exodus 3:7-8

The nation of Israel, in the midst of their oppression, cried out to God. There was an agony in their cry. In Hebrew it does not mean "the voice of their prayer or penance," but it means "the cry of their agony." The people were so oppressed that they could not articulate their hurt to ask God to set them free. They were so deeply oppressed by their taskmasters that when they went to God, there was only a moaning that came out of them.

When people pray like that, others may think they are crazy. Though no one understands what is said, God understands the language of the moan. Most of us cannot interpret moans, even when people are speaking in English. But, God hears the moan and reads the heart that sent the message, even before the voice cries out with intelligible words. God listened to the heart of the people who were the descendants of those with whom He cut covenant; He remembered the covenant He made with Abraham, Isaac and Jacob.

Our problem is that we cannot interpret the moan. Not only that, but we are bothered by the moaning of the people. The Church does not want to hear it. But, if the Church does not hear the moans, it will never take time to interpret the feeling behind the moans. The cry of the oppressed is not a cry for candy, it is a cry for mercy.

Parents understand their children's moans. There are times when babies cry just because they feel like crying. Parents have the ability to endure it because they know babies need to cry a little bit. But, there is also a cry when babies are sick or something is wrong. They are not able to say, "Mommy, my tummy hurts," so they cry in a certain way, and parents go to the crib very quickly. This is how God understood the children of Israel. He heard a cry that was not a cry for candy; He heard a moan for mercy. God began to respond to the agony of oppression upon the Israelites. He heard a cry, and His heart and ear tuned in, and His feet began to move. How was it that God's feet began to move? He sent Moses into Egypt.

God is hearing the groaning of the oppressed in this country, and He is looking for some feet. God is looking for a man. "And I sought for a man among them, that should make up the hedge, and stand in the gap before Me for the land, that I should not destroy it: but I found none" (Ezek. 22:30). When God's ears are open to our moan, He is moved to work and live through somebody in order to reach those who are hurting and those who are oppressed.

It is very easy to sit back and do nothing, but that perpetuates oppression. The Church may not be oppressors, but we are called to loose those who are oppressed. We cannot stand to the side and say, "I am not oppressing anybody, so everything is okay." No, everything is not okay.

God is concerned about the city and the people in the city who are dying in their sins. Some people use drugs because they believe there is nothing else that will give them a few minutes' relief from the oppression of the ghetto. This is not to condone drug use, but people could be sensitive enough to understand that the poor take a little trip out of the ghetto through drugs.

God heard the cry that came from those who were oppressed in Israel. The apostle Paul heard the cry of oppression from a people who lived in a place we now call Europe. These people had never heard the gospel, but Paul heard their cry calling him to where they were. Church, we need to hear the cry of the hurting, oppressed, poor, forgotten and overlooked people of our society.

Do we hear the cry of those on whom the world has given up, those who the world says are no good? Do we believe that Jesus died for those who supposedly will never amount to anything? Do we believe there is a cry that God wants us to hear? Do we believe God is telling the Church to be quiet for a moment, to still our hearts and hear the cry that He hears?

The Person Whom God Selects

Once God sees the oppression of a people He desires to set free, He selects a person to be His instrument. Could it be that this is why so much oppression has been permitted in North America, South America and Central America?

Most of us would not like to be a black person living under the conditions of those in South Africa. This oppression is no less than what the Jews experienced in Egypt: people do laborious work and receive no pay. Others become multimillionaires because of those who work for no pay. People do not like to be told that they have to go to the back of the bus, that they have to drink from a different water fountain, that they have to use different bathrooms or that they cannot live in certain areas and are forced to live in bad areas.

Who cries out for these oppressed people? Sure, clergymen are crying out, but most of these people do not even know God. Yet, we who know God are letting people who do not know Him cry out about those things for which God would cry out. What has happened to us?

God has been "burning in a bush," and He cannot find anyone who will stop and look. We do not want to look at the bush, because it is a humble bush. But, the God who created the earth and everything in it chose to reveal Himself in a lowly bush.

The Church today is so overwhelmed with opulence and prosperity that when God reveals Himself, all most of us see is a fire. Moses stopped and he saw God. God is looking for someone who will stop by that bush and say, "God is trying to get my attention." There have been many bushes burning in front of us, and we have not seen them.

Still God chooses human creation to fulfill His purpose and will. "And I sought for a man among them, that should make up the hedge, and stand in the gap before Me for the land, that I should not destroy it: but I found none"

(Ezek. 22:30). In this verse of Scripture we find the greatest manhunt, the greatest mission and the greatest misfortune— God found none to stand in the gap.

A burden is a vision, and without it, people perish. God chooses men with burdens. Moses was a man with a burden, who at times demonstrated it in drastic ways. Once he killed an Egyptian. It was wrong for Moses to kill the man, but it demonstrates the fact that he had a burden. Romans 9:1-3 tells us that Paul had a burden. Nehemiah also had a burden. Several of the minor prophets start their books with "And the burden of the Lord...." But, unlike the prophets of old, we in the Church today only think about the blessing of the Lord. God is looking for people with burdens that He has placed upon them.

Can the Church handle the burden or is the blessing of God all that we want? Is it that we will only see God in the bush when there are blessings? Will we see God only when there are hundred dollar bills on the bush that are not consumed while the bush is burning? Then would we say, "Look at this, God is here"? God did not reveal dollars to Moses, He revealed deliverance for Israel. When God reveals Himself to us, He must know that there are people who will take His burden and share it.

Our society has gone downhill because the Church is only looking uphill. We do not want to look down at God in the lowly places. God chose a man with a burden, but He also chose a method—the bush. God chose the bush as the instrument through which He brought Moses a revelation of Himself. Through the bush, God revealed to Moses that He is an all-consuming fire. This revelation came to Moses at the place where he prayed. "Now Moses kept the flock of Jethro his father in law, the priest of Midian: and he led the flock to the backside of the desert, and came to the mountain of God, even to Horeb" (Exod. 3:1). Moses was going up the mountain to pray. When people are in the spirit, God will reveal Himself to them.

Many have tremendous difficulty hearing what God is saying, because they are not going to the "mountain of prayer." A person can read all the books he wants about how to find God, how to get revelation from God and how to know what God is saying, but it is at the mountain of prayer that God will reveal Himself. It was when Peter and John were on their way to the temple to pray that the power of God came over them, and they healed the lame man. We in the Church are not being found in the grace of God or with the power of God that comes through prayer. In the attitude of prayer, tremendous things will happen. "...the people that do know their God shall be strong, and do exploits" (Dan. 11:32).

The Purpose for Which God Saves

God's intention for Israel well exceeded their deliverance; it included their duty. Christians seem to only understand deliverance. We understand that God has set us free, but we do not think too much about why God has set us free.

What is the purpose of our salvation other than being set free and going to Heaven someday? Is there a reason for salvation? Yes, there is a reason. God has a job for each one of us to do; this is why He has set us free. Once we are delivered by God, we have a duty to God.

It was from Egypt that Moses came, and it was to Egypt that God called him. Whom did God call? He called the one who had been in Egypt. Moses had been part of the hierarchy in Egypt. What Christians generally want to do is run out of the city (Egypt) and away from the burdens. We want someone else who knows nothing about the city and the urban experience to take our place. This may be very convenient for us, but it does not work, because this is not God's intention.

God wants to take the lowly and lift them up. Some may say this is prejudice, but it's not; it is biblical. God uses foolish things of the world to confound the wise. This is not to say that God does not call rich or intelligent people. He certainly does, but not to the exclusion of other people. However, when God needs a man to go to Egypt, and God finds a man who was in Egypt, He is going to call that man to go back to Egypt. Whether we like it or not, this is God's general pattern. God is sovereign, and sometimes He does it another way, but it is not His pattern to do so.

God took Moses back to Egypt because Moses knew all about Pharaoh. In fact, this is probably why Moses didn't want to go. He knew that Pharaoh would not listen to God. Even though that may have been Moses' thinking, God still was determined to show Moses His power. It was not God's intention to teach Moses how to kill the Egyptians with his hands, rather how to set the Israelites free by the almighty hand of God.

Moses had had this burden all of the time, he just did not know what to do with it. When God sent Moses back to Egypt, He did not send him with an instrument of violence, but with a rod. Nor did Moses go back in his own might, rather with God's miracles.

Lazarus was raised from the dead by the resurrection and life of Jesus Christ. But, when Lazarus arose bound by his grave clothes, Jesus told those close by to loose him and let him go. God always uses a human instrument to set free and deliver.

Is the Church ready to go to Pharaoh, or are we afraid of Pharaoh? The Church is afraid of Pharaoh, and it is even trying to make alliance and agreement with Pharaoh. We are trying to become a part of the system. But, people do not change an evil system by becoming evil. People change an evil system by standing against the system. It's tiring to hear people say that it's necessary to become a part of the system in order to change the system. Moses was taken out of the system to go back and speak out against the system. We do not need to go into the system in order to make the necessary changes. If people want to change things by their own might, then they have to go into the system. But, when people want to change things through the miracles of God, they can stand outside the system and cry out against it.

Christians tend not to cry out against the system; we seem to be very happy with the system. But, God is calling us to go to "Pharaoh." God is telling us to go to the devil and say, "Let God's people go." God is calling us to stand against crack and say, "Let God's people go." God is looking for people who will step right up against AIDS and say, "Let God's people go." God wants us to stand against heroin and say, "Let God's people go." God wants us to go into the midst of those who are bound by materialism and say, "Let God's people go."

We have been set free so that we might proclaim the Lord, not so that we will become a part of the system. The system has a problem with Jerry Kaufman and Love Gospel Assembly. It does not like anybody outside the system. But, there never was a prophet, in either the Old or New Testament, who was popular in society. There were false prophets owned by the people, but the real prophets owed nothing to anyone. They had only God. They were a special group who knew how to suffer and were willing to suffer, because the Word and the burden of the Lord were strong in their lives.

When Moses went to Pharaoh, Pharaoh said, "Who sent you?" He wanted to know if Moses had been sent by a king or an ambassador. Moses knew that Pharaoh would ask this question, so Moses had asked God, "Who should I say sent me?" God had said, "I Am sent you. I am that I am." Thus, when Moses went to Pharaoh, he did not say, "The Lord sent me." He did not say, "Love (or Liberty) sent me." He said, "I Am sent me." The *I Am* to whom Moses referred is the One who created the heavens and the earth. He is the *I Am* of Abraham, Isaac and Jacob.

When we go to "Pharaoh," there is only One who can send us, and that is the *I Am*. When we go, saying, "I, a church, a denomination or a mission board sent me," we are in for a lot of trouble. When we face "Pharaoh," we have to say, "God sent me. Here I am."

But, people do not like that. In taking this strong attitude because we are sent by God a person will have to deal with being called arrogant. But, this is not arrogance. When a person speaks out of God's commissioning, it is because he is enlightened. These individuals are no more arrogant than Moses was when he faced Pharaoh and said that he was going to take the people out of Egypt. Moses knew who had sent him. We need to know who is sending us. We need to proclaim, "The Lord sent me."

Now, the young "whippersnappers" should not go until God sends them. "God sent me" is not a cliché, and it should not be used as such. Remember, a few people tried to cast out a devil, and the demons said, "Jesus we know, and Paul we know, but who are you?" We must remember this verse of Scripture when we start to get ahead of ourselves and think that we're more than God has made us to be. The devil will ask, "Who are you?"

One of the purposes God has for us is to proclaim the Lord, but the second purpose is to possess the land. "Also I brought you up from the land of Egypt, and led you forty years through the wilderness, to possess the land of the Amorite" (Amos 2:10). God brought the Israelites up from the land of Egypt to possess the land. He led them 40 years to finally give them the land He had covenanted to give to their forefathers, Abraham, Isaac and Jacob.

God frees us from oppression for a purpose. Some people think they came out of a lifestyle of drug abuse just to be set free from drugs. Yes, God did do that, but that's not all. The purpose of being set free from drugs is not just to stand up and give a testimony and be nice people. God calls us to proclaim the Lord and possess the land.

God is looking for deliverers today. God wants His people to be instruments of freedom and a voice of conscience to the Body of Christ. People may not like us, because we're shaking their comfortable nests. We may be asked, "Who do you think you are?" because we are not allowing them to go on with "church as usual." But, we will not just sit around seeing only blessings in the bush and not burdens in the bush. It is time for the bush to burn, and it is time for that bush to burn a burden into our spirit.

Oppression is rampant. People are being squeezed and stepped on. They have taskmasters who drive them. When people are oppressed, it is as though they are driven by an army to the slaughter. This is what was done to Jesus, as prophesied in Isaiah 53:7.

But, if we study oppression and then try to solve the problems of oppression with hands that hold machine guns and with the strength of human power, we're in trouble. Where will it end?

Most of those who are oppressed become oppressors. Then, someone comes behind them with the same machine gun they laid down when they attained the throne of power, and that same machine gun used to shoot and kill the oppressor contains the bullets that will be used against them.

The only way out of oppression is for God to raise up deliverers to set the oppressed free. People need to be taught that their purpose in life is not to become the oppressors, but the liberators of the oppressed. This is where we've failed. When we do not put a sense of duty into those who have been delivered, they will put other people into bondage.

God is the God of the oppressed! Those who have gone out from Love Gospel Assembly, whether it was to Orlando's inner city, to Mexico, to Puerto Rico, to Boston, or to Barbados, will not join the system. They will speak against the system as God leads them.

Chapter Seven

The Year of Jubilee

The spirit of the Lord is upon Me, because He hath anointed Me to preach the gospel to the poor; He hath sent Me to heal the brokenhearted, to preach deliverance to the captives, and recovering of sight to the blind, to set at liberty them that are bruised, to preach the acceptable year of the Lord.

Luke 4:18-19

Luke 4:18 is incomplete without Luke 4:19. The word *preach* is just like the term *preach deliverance*; it does not mean "preach," as we know it, it means "proclaim." It can be compared to the sounding of a trumpet. When we read "...to preach the acceptable year of the Lord," it really means "to proclaim the year of God's favor." This unquestionably speaks about the year of jubilee.

For the Israelites, the year of jubilee was the 50th year of a cycle, and its expression was threefold. First of all, there was a release from bondage; slaves were set free. Secondly, the people of Israel returned to their possessions. If someone had been given a piece of land when Joshua went into Canaan, during the 50th years, no matter what had happened to that land in the meantime, it was given back to that person's descendants. So, there was a restoration. Thirdly, there was a rest for the land. In the 50th year, nothing was to be planted and nothing was to be harvested.

In the 50th year there was not supposed to be any planting of seed nor toiling on the land. The greatest thing that can happen to a piece of land is that periodically it is given rest. The question is, "How will we survive the seventh and eighth years?" The answer is that in the sixth year God will give a harvest big enough to carry us through the next two years.

Rest is very different from what we understand in our contemporary society. In doing a study on the word *clay*, one would find that once a potter had pounded the clay, he would stop and give it rest. Clay has no life in it, yet it needs rest so the potter can continue pounding.

Our concept of rest is that we work from 9 to 5, Monday through Friday, and then cease from all the work we did. This is not the biblical concept of rest. The biblical concept is that we take rest so we can work more fruitfully. Many of us are not fruitful in our work because we rest *from* work, not *to* work.

"...To preach the acceptable year of the Lord." In the context from which Luke 4:19 is taken, Isaiah 61, the passage says, "...to proclaim...the day of vengeance of our God...." Why did Luke leave *vengeance* out? The vengeance of which God was speaking in Isaiah 61 was against the enemies of Zion. To His people God proclaimed a year of His favor, a year of jubilee. To the enemies of His people God announced that vengeance was coming. In Jesus Christ there are no earthly enemies of God's people, because God, in Christ, died for all. Therefore, the poor, the broken-hearted, the captives, the blind, the oppressed, and all people are the people that God wants to reach. God is speaking of "total jubilee." He is not looking for vengeance, He is looking to give restoration and rest to His people. If the word *vengeance* was included in this verse of Scripture, it would be bad for the Gentiles. In Jesus there is no vengeance toward the Gentiles or the outsiders.

The context of both Isaiah 61 and Luke 4 indicates that Jesus has come to preach to the poor, heal the broken-hearted, preach deliverance to the captives, open the eyes of the blind, set at liberty the oppressed and proclaim a year of jubilee for all. The year of jubilee has come to all who are poor, to all who are slaves, to all who do not have anything and to all those who are bound.

God's instructions for the year of jubilee are found in the Book of Leviticus:

And thou shalt number seven sabbaths of years unto thee, seven times seven years; and the space of the seven sabbaths of years shall be unto thee forty and nine years. Then shalt thou cause the trumpet of the jubilee to sound on the tenth day of the seventh month, in the day of atonement shall ye make the trumpet sound throughout all your land. And ye shall hallow the fiftieth year, and proclaim liberty through-out all the land unto all the inhabitants thereof: it shall be a jubilee unto you; and ye shall return every

*man unto his possession, and ye shall return every
man unto his family.*

Leviticus 25:8-10

We read in these verses that there is a trumpet, but it is not the trumpet for the rapture, it is a trumpet of release. It is not a trumpet for us to escape, but it is a trumpet to signify that we are to be edified.

The whole concept of the year of jubilee is designed for the poor. It is not for the rich; in fact, the rich do not like jubilee because it is during this time that they have to give back some of their wealth. This special feast is for those who are described in Luke 4:18.

When did the jubilee start? In the 50th year, at the beginning of the Jewish year, on the first day of Rosh Hashanah, the effects of jubilee would begin. The slaves, although not yet allowed to return home to the possessions that would be theirs, no longer had to serve their owners. On that first day, the slaves were set free. They could sit, eat, drink and be merry. Not only that, but they were also to wear crowns on their heads. To those who were slaves and to those who were poor, it was a time of great release and blessing.

The slaves would sit for ten days. Because Rosh Hashanah and Yom Kippur are ten days apart. Freedom could not happen until the Day of Atonement (Yom Kippur). On the tenth day the high priest would walk into the holy of holies to offer sacrifices for himself and the nation, and at the end of the day, the trumpet would sound.

The New Testament reveals that the sacrifice has already been made. Jesus went into the holy of holies in order to usher in a jubilee that the world had never known. What did Jesus do on the cross? He "blew a trumpet." Today, there are people who are listening for the trumpet that calls us out of bondage. We need to be listening for that trumpet that says the streets are ours. The Day of Atonement has already come. Now is the year of jubilee.

God is going to blow a different trumpet. He is going to blow a trumpet to let the cities of this world know that He has come to set them free. The atonement has come; it is already the tenth day. Now, we can go home and receive our possessions. We are not playing church anymore. God is doing something new. There is no more "church as usual." It is time to drop the traditions. The trumpet has sounded. The trumpet of Jesus Christ is saying, "I send forth a feast into the land." There is a release from the slavery that poverty brings (when a person is poor, he ends up being somebody's slave). This *year of jubilee* is a release, and it is also a rest.

Isaiah 61:3 speaks of mourning, of being in the ashes. There is a spirit of heaviness. In this jubilee we are no longer in the ashes, in mourning and having a spirit of heaviness. For ashes, God gives beauty; for mourning, He gives the oil of joy; and He gives us rest for the spirit of heaviness by putting the garments of praise on us.

"They shall build the old wastes, they shall raise up the former desolations, and they shall repair the waste cities, the desolation of many generations" (Isa. 61:4). Many people want us to believe that this verse speaks of the millennium. This is because those who maintain that view do not live in waste places. They do not know that the waste places need to be built now. God is doing something new, now.

The trumpet has sounded. The Day of Atonement has come. Now, we can possess what belongs to us. What does belong to us? The cities of the world. New York City belongs to us. Tokyo belongs to us. Orlando belongs to us. Barbados belongs to us. Now that we have heard the trumpet, we are going to go and possess the cities of this world. The Church in this world has not claimed them, but we *must* claim them. The Body of Christ has claimed riches and gold, now we must claim the poor and the outcast of this world.

Epilogue

He hath shewed thee, O man, what is good; and what doth the Lord require of thee, but to do justly, and to love mercy, and to walk humbly with thy God?

Micah 6:8

It is impossible to preach about the poor without addressing our responsibility to fulfill the Word of the Lord. It is easy for me to understand why the children of Israel wanted to go back to Egypt; they did not want the responsibility of Canaan land. They were more willing to be slaves, than soldiers. They were more interested in being governed, than in governing. Some of us will stay in menial jobs for the rest of our lives, even though we are capable of handling more difficult jobs. We do not want the responsibility. However, responsibility will not kill us. Instead, it will develop and refine our capabilities. The people who need to be in responsible positions in this world are Christians who can successfully do the work these positions require.

I can understand why we really don't want the move of God in our churches or why we want God to move slowly.

The more God speaks to us, the more responsible we become. We can ignore God's will, but we cannot run from our responsibility to fulfill it. Once we hear from God, He holds us responsible for what He has put in our spirit. Presently, we are more responsible to the Lord than we have ever been. We are also more responsible to those whom God loves.

I admit that Love Gospel Assembly is more responsible for the poor than most churches in this country because we have been exposed to so much of what the Bible says about the poor. Other churches know little about the poor because they have not received enough teaching on this issue. God will judge Love Gospel Assembly in relation to what we know and what we do.

Let us examine four responsibilities to the poor: First, we must recognize their condition. Second, we must consider restoring the captives. Third, we must consider reacting to the curse (there is a curse in this land, and we need to learn what to do about it). Fourth, we will consider the rebuilding of the cities.

Recognizing Their Condition; Weeping to God

In the Book of Nehemiah, we find an example of someone weeping to God.

The words of Nehemiah the son of Hachaliah. And it came to pass in the month Chisleu, in the twentieth year, as I was in Shushan the palace, that Hanani, one of my brethren, came, he and certain men of Judah; and I asked them concerning the Jews that had escaped, which were left of the captivity, and concerning Jerusalem. And they said unto me, The remnant that are left of the captivity there in the province are in great affliction and reproach: the wall of Jerusalem also is broken down, and the gates thereof are burned with fire.

Nehemiah 1:1-3

Nehemiah is a man not only to be admired, but also to be followed. He was overwhelmed with concern for his people and their captivity, even though their situation did not affect him personally. Nehemiah was very far away from their captivity, yet he could not bear the news about his people's reproach and afflictions.

Nehemiah wept when he recognized the condition of the people. The Israelites had no protection, water or food. Nehemiah was not only concerned about the captives who were having struggles, but he was also concerned about those who had been freed from captivity. He was concerned about God's people. Unfortunately, there are very few Christians who want to recognize the condition of the poor and weep to God about it.

I have become so annoyed with people who have come off drugs and then will not do anything to help another addict find God. Many of them have gone through Christian drug programs, yet they never send donations to help those ministries to remain in existence.

What was the condition of the Israelites? They were in a terrible state of sin. They went into Babylonian captivity because they had rebelled against God. Rebellion was and still is a stench to the nostrils of God.

We must not rebel against God's plan to reach the poor. We need to recognize that the poor are sinners who need the Lord in order to get out of their condition. We must reach out to them with the gospel of Jesus Christ. God does not want the poor to stay in captivity. What are we going to do with those who are captives? Do we just sit back and allow them to remain in that condition, or do we take the burden as Nehemiah did for the Israelites?

It is our responsibility to recognize the condition of the poor and to weep for them. In addition, we must provide for their needs once they have come out of captivity. When I came out of captivity, I needed someone to strengthen me in my new state of liberty. I believe we need to build strong churches so that those coming out of captivity can find security in the house of God. When I was on drugs, I used to roam the streets day and night, but once God saved me, I could no longer live like that. Someone had to help create a place for me.

There are many members of the Body of Christ who condemn the poor people in the city, claiming they are just lazy. Obviously, there are some lazy poor people, but there also are some who are not lazy. They are hurting people who need the gospel of Jesus Christ.

Restoring the Captives: The Will of God

We must become involved in restoring the lives of the poor. The prophet Isaiah dealt with a people who had sinned and become captives as a result of their sins.

But this is a people robbed and spoiled; they are all of them snared in holes, and they are hid in prison

*houses: they are for a prey, and none delivereth; for
a spoil, and none saith, Restore.*

Isaiah 42:22

It was obvious that the people had sinned, and they were imprisoned because of that sin. Nevertheless, God was annoyed that there was no one willing to restore them.

We have learned about the imprisonment of the poor, needy and anguished. We have learned about the effects of oppression. Now, we have the responsibility of restoring the people. God is calling us to bring restoration to a captive and abused group of people. Our society will stop condemning poor people when they discover that the poor have someone who stands with them.

What does restoring the captives include? First of all, it includes a willingness to speak up for them. "Open thy mouth for the dumb in the cause of all such as are appointed to destruction. Open thy mouth, judge righteously, and plead the cause of the poor and needy" (Prov. 31:8-9). To whom is God speaking? He is speaking to His people. We must be willing to speak for those who are being held captive. There needs to be a willingness to stand up for them. In Isaiah 42:22, God says that no one was standing up for those who were in captivity.

When society sees that the Church really cares for hurting people and is willing to work with them and house them, it will turn them over to us.

Reacting to the Curse: Worship of God

Our responsibility to the poor is also to react to the curse. Sin and rebellion produce a curse or plague. In Numbers 16 we read the story of Korah and other leaders in Israel who rebelled against God's authority. Israel continued to rebel and resist God's authority, and eventually, a curse (or plague) spread throughout the camp.

> *But on the morrow all the congregation of the children of Israel murmured against Moses and against Aaron, saying, Ye have killed the people of the Lord. And it came to pass, when the congregation was gathered against Moses and against Aaron, that they looked toward the tabernacle of the congregation: and, behold, the cloud covered it, and the glory of the Lord appeared. And Moses and Aaron came before the tabernacle of the congregation.*
>
> *And the Lord spake unto Moses, saying, Get you up from among this congregation, that I may consume them as in a moment. And they fell upon their faces.*

Numbers 16:41-45

The reason for the curse was Israel's resistance to God's authority. Interestingly, Moses and Aaron stopped that plague. Aaron began to burn incense and make atonement for the people (Numbers 16:46). We know that incense represents praise and worship offered to the Lord. As Aaron, the high priest, worshiped and as the incense rose up to God, the sins of the people were covered.

Where did Aaron worship? Moses did not tell Aaron to worship in the holy place or next to the veil, which was where they generally burned the incense. Moses told Aaron to go out to where the people were. Similarly, in order to stop the curse or plague in this nation, we must go out to the people and "burn incense and make atonement for them."

Many Christians believe that AIDS is a plague or a curse in our society. It is rampant in the inner city and among IV drug users. When we go to the streets, there will be times when we preach, and there will also be times when we worship. Some people may not like it, but they do not understand that we will be holding plagues back. We must worship God in spirit and in truth so that the blood of Jesus can cover our sins and stop the curse before it destroys us.

Rebuilding the Cities: Wall of God

The last responsibility to the poor is the rebuilding of the cities. Once we have recognized the condition of the poor, restored the captives and reacted to the curse, what will we do with the poor who do not have decent housing? What does God require of us? We must rebuild the city and not run away from the city. We need to make room for the harvest that is coming.

In spite of the difficulties and opposition, Nehemiah was determined to rebuild the wall for the benefit of the Jews who had returned to Jerusalem.

But it came to pass, that when Sanballat heard that we builded the wall, he was wroth, and took great indignation, and mocked the Jews. And he spake before his brethren and the army of Samaria, and said, What do these feeble Jews? will they fortify themselves? will they sacrifice? will they make an end in a day? will they revive the stones out of the heaps of the rubbish which are burned? Now Tobiah the Ammonite was by him, and he said, Even that which they build, if a fox go up, he shall even break down their stone

wall. Hear, O our God; for we are despised: and turn
their reproach upon their own head, and give them
for a prey in the land of captivity: And cover not their
iniquity, and let not their sin be blotted out from be-
fore Thee: for they have provoked Thee to anger be-
fore the builders.

Nehemiah 4:1-5

Sanballat and Tobiah were astounded that Nehemiah was going to build the wall with burnt stones. Yet, Nehemiah was able to knit together those burnt stones to rebuild the wall around the city and provide protection for his people. Speaking from a spiritual perspective, we can say that we were once burnt stones, and God wants us to be united in order to rebuild the cities, so that the needs of the poor and oppressed can be met.

It is God's will to build a wall around the city so that the world can no longer touch it, so that when people come out of captivity, we will not have to weep and say, "Where will they go?" Instead, we will be able to provide a place for the poor, for the needy and for the oppressed.

So built we the wall; and all the wall was joined to-
gether unto the half thereof: for the people had a
mind to work.

Nehemiah 4:6

A Capsule of Our Community

The Love Kitchen

To understand the Love Kitchen, you have to understand this community. In a local newspaper the sanitation department was quoted as saying, "This community is the dirtiest community in New York City." As you walk around the streets, you see garbage all over the sidewalks. In front of stores, early in the morning, you see people picking through the garbage to see if they can find something of value. Alcoholics, drug addicts and the desperate go through garbage bags looking for beer and soda cans which they can redeem for five cents. Around here you see graffiti all over the buildings and blobs of chewing gum all over the sidewalks. The sidewalks of our community are freckled with gum.

The street behind our church is an open-air drug market, operating 24 hours a day, seven days a week. Our church is side-by-side with a pornographic theater, where prostitutes and homosexuals service the clientele of that establishment. On the other side of our church is a welfare hotel for transients, in which drugs, prostitution, stealing, fights, arguments and decadence are a way of life. Enter at your own risk! Many enter that hotel looking for action or a convenient place for a tryst. There are two other such hotels within two blocks of our church.

Our community has many abandoned and burnt-out buildings. We have a massive number of welfare recipients, high school dropouts, fatherless children, drug addicts, "crackheads," illegal aliens, substandard schools, prostitutes, homeless people, unemployed, ad infinitum. If there is anything negative that has not been mentioned, we probably have that, too.

The greatest number of people who have AIDS in New York City live in this community. We also have the greatest number of babies born with AIDS. The people of this community live life at its primitive level. They like amusement, movies, TV, entertainment, ambulance chasing, fire watching, shoot-outs, street fights, sports and watching people get arrested. They love the heroes of the pop culture.

Many people around here love to "rip off" the government. They believe they are "getting over." In reality they are at the bottom of the barrel in our society. They serve as fodder for a vast bureaucracy which thrives and continues to grow at the expense of the taxpayer. Our community generates a tremendous number of jobs for Social Service agencies, the Welfare Department, rehabilitation centers, correctional institutions, educational programs, ad finitum.

There is no respect or courtesy in the streets. The basic philosophy is the survival of the fittest. If you go anywhere outside our church, you might be shot and killed. These are some of the most dangerous streets in New York City.

If being at the bottom of the totem pole is not bad enough, we also have the problem of racism in this community. The newly arrived African blacks, the blacks from the Caribbean and the native American blacks do not get along. Spanish-speaking people from different countries do not like each other. The blacks and Hispanics blame their ills and troubles on "society" (the white people). Then, they turn around and harm each other the way they say "society" is doing to them. People in this community are not only racist and bigoted, they also are as exploitative as "society." Yet, nobody addresses this issue.

If that is not enough, our community is also very macho. Women are considered to be less valuable than men. They command no respect and suffer verbal abuse and harassment as they walk through our streets. The woman's lot in life is to serve a sexual function and bring up fatherless children. They have to stand in welfare lines and beg to have basic necessities provided.

One of Love Gospel Assembly's answers to some of the problems that plague our community is the Love Kitchen. The Love Kitchen is open Monday through Friday from 11:30 a.m. to 1:30 p.m. to feed the adults and from 2:30 to 3:30 p.m. to feed the children when they are dismissed from school.

The Love Kitchen is funded by the people of our congregation. There is only one paid staff member; the rest of the people are volunteers from our congregation and community. All are welcome to come to the Love Kitchen and have a meal in a warm, safe environment.

The people who come to the Love Kitchen are expected to conduct themselves like ladies and gentlemen. Unruly behavior is not tolerated. There is no harassment of women; they are to be treated like ladies, even if they are prostitutes. People are not allowed to make fun of alcoholics, homosexuals, the homeless, the mentally retarded, the poor, the destitute, the exconvict, people with AIDS or anybody else. All people are treated with respect; nothing less is acceptable.

The Love Kitchen requires hard work. Before the doors are opened, there is much preparation involved. The place must be neat, clean and in right order—for our guests. The preparation begins at 9 a.m. with the hauling of supplies, washing, cooking, cleaning, opening of many cans and taking out of the garbage. It is like working in a restaurant, and we aim to give the best service.

The people who come to the Love Kitchen are served their food as they sit, as in a restaurant. The reason for such service is that it gives dignity to those who are beaten by the streets. The only requirements we make of the people who come to eat is that they take their paper dishes and plastic forks to the trash can.

There is no smoking or cursing tolerated in the Love Kitchen. Bullies in this community do not dominate or control any aspect of our atmosphere; we set the standard and the tone of our operation. Thus, the women and children and the weaker, timid people feel safe from the marauders of our community. They know we will fight to protect them. They have been discarded, disrespected, disillusioned and dumped on, but God wants to take away these hurts and replace them with deliverance in our sanctuary and dignity in our Love Kitchen.

The Love Kitchen is a type of sanctuary. It is a place of refuge in a hostile environment. We pray for the people. We counsel them. We also refer people to other ministries within our church. By doing that, we enable the people to get the help they need. Through the Love Kitchen we make the community aware of other resources that are available to them: shelters, legal aid, government aid, alcohol and drug programs, educational and medical agencies.

We have established long-term relationships within this community. We let the people know that this is their church, and we are here to help them in any way we can. We know these people. We welcome them, accept them and above all, love them. Love lifts, and that is the basic reason for the Love Kitchen.

Meals Served

1984	71,527
1985	95,303
1986	108,159
1987	103,571
1988	105,346
1989	118,872
1990	145,000
1991	128,771
1992	111,628
Total	**998,177**

Feb. '93   1 millionth meal

Montefiore Hospital

Many people in our community do not have any form of identification, so the bureaucracy refuses to service them. These are the people who fall through the cracks in our society.

Montefiore Hospital provides health care for the homeless every Monday and Wednesday in the Love Kitchen. The Montefiore health team consists of a nurse practitioner, psychiatric nurse, social worker and administrative assistant. Sometimes the medical doctor accompanies the team.

The nurse examines them and prescribes medication for minor ailments. The more severe cases are referred to hospitals where there is immediate admittance, even for those without identification. The psychiatric nurse helps those with drug, alcohol and mental problems. The social worker advises people about food stamps, welfare, social benefits and/or medical services available to the community. The administrative assistant keeps the records of all transactions between the medical team and the clients, which provides for continuity of care.

Care Services

In response to the leading of God, the Care Services opened their doors about 12 years ago. The Care Services of Love Gospel Assembly are an integral part of the vision, philosophy and overall ministry of our church. As such, these services are geared toward the various spiritual, psychological, social and economic needs of the oppressed in our community. In conjunction with the preaching and teaching ministries of our church, the Care Services provide the practical expression of the gospel of Jesus Christ.

The initial services provided were the distribution of nonperishable food items, crisis counseling and information and referral services. Since the inception of Care Services, the needs of the community have drastically changed, creating the need to expand services provided to the community. We now face a multiplicity of problems, including the disintegration of the family, AIDS, homelessness, destitute senior citizens, teenage pregnancies, gang rapes, the crack epidemic, child abuse, family violence, loss of cultural pride among black and other minority men, the increase in the practice of cultural religions involving witchcraft, drug abuse among the mentally ill, incest and blatant homosexuality. In order to deal more effectively with these problems, the following services were implemented:

1. Food pantry
2. Counseling
3. Shelter referral service
4. Substance abuse crisis intervention and referral services
5. Job training and literacy program referral services
6. Legal advocacy
7. Clothing distribution

Explanation of Services

Food Pantry

This is a voluntary, non-government-funded program which is sponsored by the members of our church, who donate food and money for distribution to the community.

These funds and donations are the only source which makes possible the purchase of food to help feed the poor.

The Food Pantry operates from Monday through Friday from 10 a.m. to 4 p.m. We currently have five volunteers who are responsible for the daily functions of this program. Their duties include maintaining the inventory for the food pantry, gathering statistics and conducting an initial assessment of clients, as well as the actual distribution of food items.

Last year the Food Pantry distributed approximately 200,000 food items and serviced 20,000 people. Currently, the Food Pantry provides upwards of 450 individuals and families with a food package on a weekly basis.

As an example of the services provided by the Food Pantry, we have included a case history of a client serviced by this program.

Case History

Mrs. M. is a black, middle-aged mother of five who came to us for food for her family. At the interview, it was discovered that this woman was in deep turmoil. Mrs. M. told us that her husband of 17 years had recently been removed from their home after raping their 15-year-old daughter. This crisis had caused a great financial and emotional burden on the family.

The disintegration of the family had caused great emotional turmoil for her children, which was manifested in nightmares and suicidal ideation. In addition, this woman's husband placed a heavy burden of guilt on her by threatening to commit suicide as well.

We provided Mrs. M. with spiritual and emotional support and a food package. After assessing this client's need for further services, we referred her to Victim Services Agency. This agency provides many services, including family counseling. Mrs. M. was followed up and reports about her are hopeful at this time.

Counseling Services

Counseling is available Monday through Friday from 9 a.m. to 5 p.m. Counseling services are provided on a walk-in and/or telephone call-in basis. These services are crisis oriented and include information and referral services, as needed. Counseling is provided on a short-term, individual basis. Upwards of 100 clients per month utilize these services.

The primary motive in providing this service is ultimately evangelism.

The following case histories are examples of situations which have actually occurred among clients seeking our services.

Case History No. 1

Ms. J. is a black, 30-year-old incest survivor, who was raised by her paternal grandmother in Jamaica until the age of nine. Upon her grandmother's death, this client was sent to New York by the court system in Jamaica to meet and live with her biological parents. When the client arrived in New York, her parents' whereabouts were unknown. Ms. J. was placed in the care of the Child Welfare Administration.

Shortly after placement, Ms. J.'s father was located, and custody was awarded to him. After placement with her father, the client reports having been raped by him and then removed and placed again in the care of the CWA. Due to rape trauma, Ms. J. became a selective mute, causing her condition to be misdiagnosed, and she was placed in a mental institution. At some point during her stay, she began to regain her ability to speak. Upon reaching her 18th birthday, she became old enough to leave and was referred to a drug program because further placement could not be arranged for her. There she became introduced to the drug culture. It was also there that Ms. J. met her first husband.

In that marriage Ms. J. was subjected to emotional and financial abuse, which caused the marriage to end in divorce. She then became homeless and was involved in the shelter system, where she met and then married a Black Muslim who sexually abused her.

Alone again, the woman then came to the Care Services for help and was offered spiritual and emotional support. This client presented a fearful disposition and initially would not allow the worker near her. After the worker convinced Ms. J. to pray with her, she became relaxed and allowed us to help her work out her problems.

We referred her to the Montefiore health team for the homeless for a physical examination and psychiatric assessment, provided her with clothing and helped her secure housing. The woman was followed up by our workers, and she is now being properly cared for and attends a local church.

Case History No. 2

Mr. L. is a young Hispanic male who was born in the United States and raised in Spain by his mother and stepfather. The client reports having been sexually abused by his stepfather throughout his childhood.

Mr. L. returned to the States as a young adult and became involved in the study of karate in order to find an identity. As a competitor in championships, he enjoyed the attention he received from the crowds as he excelled in his sport.

During this time Mr. L. became sexually involved with a female intravenous drug user, who infected him with the AIDS virus. After discovering that he was HIV positive, Mr. L. became distraught and began abusing drugs himself. He then signed himself into a methadone program. When he reached us, he was on a high dosage of methadone. He was asked if he wanted our help with detoxification.

He was provided with spiritual support, invited to church and was given the opportunity to be admitted into a Christian drug program for HIV-positive exdrug users. He returned several times for short-term counseling, but never committed to entering a program.

Shelter Referral Services

This is a crisis-oriented program which screens homeless families and individuals and locates for them private shelter space. This involves placement in missions or rooms in private homes, freeing us from the bureaucracy of the public shelter systems. We service upwards of 150 clients per month.

This program has provided help to members of the community, including crisis assistance to a homeless family who was forced out of their apartment because they refused to deal drugs in their community. One of the clients in this family had severe asthma and could not remain in the shelter where they had been, due to health concerns (strong fumes near the shelter). The fumes had exacerbated the client's asthmatic condition and threatened the client's life. Intervention included advocacy with the homeless' fair hearing, which provided the client with the ability to leave the shelter for a healthier environment. We also provided spiritual and emotional support and gave her some clothing for her family and herself. The client also was provided with a food package.

Substance Abuse Crisis Intervention and Referral Services

Throughout the history of the Care Services' existence, a need for intervention with substance abusers has become more apparent. The changes in the drug culture have made it necessary to create different methods for intervening with substance abusers. We have seen a greater degree of domestic violence, an increase in drug-related crimes, broken family units as a result of the crack epidemic and an increase in child abuse and neglect. These situations have caused the Care Services to network more closely with the

Child Welfare Administration, the court system and the Social Services.

Substance abuse appears to span the generations and touches people from all walks of life. We service upwards of 125 substance abuse cases per month, and this number continues to climb daily. In addition to the above, our services provide spiritual guidance and referrals for detoxification and Christian or drug-free secular long-term residential programs.

Case History

Ms. C. is a black, 23-year-old female who is a self-proclaimed crack abuser. In order to support her habit, Ms. C. became involved in prostitution and left her child in the care of individuals whom she barely knew. They were crack users also.

Upon coming to our office, Ms. C. reported having been separated from her child for over a month. She said she had not gone back to the place where she had left the child because she was fearful of being assaulted by the people who were caring for her child.

This client reported that she was already involved with the Child Welfare Administration and was afraid of reporting to them because she thought her child might be dead. Ms. C. had another child, who had been placed in the care of her mother by CWA, and had a CWA worker already assigned to her.

The Care Service worker intervened by calling the Child Welfare Administration and speaking with her worker. The worker informed Ms. C. that if she came to the office without the child, she would be arrested. She also was told that if she gave the address where the child could be located, they would meet her there. They would then remove the child from the home, and more than likely, she still would be arrested. Upon hearing this, Ms. C. became hysterical and threatened to leave our office.

We were able to convince the CWA worker to consider a more lenient stance, if the client would pick up the child on her own and return to our office with the child. The child could then be handed over to the CWA worker. Upon agreeing with the terms, the client was provided with spiritual counseling and advised to follow through with her agreement with CWA.

Job Training and Literacy Program Referral Services

As a result of servicing the poor, the Care Services have encountered many clients with limited education and job skills. These clients are referred to job training and literacy training programs in order to upgrade their skills and increase their feeling of self-worth and self-esteem.

Most of these programs provide clients with a stipend to help defer carfare and lunch expenses. They are purposely designed to help these clients become tax-paying citizens. At present, we service upwards of 80 clients per month who require this service.

Telephone Counseling and Prayer Services

Telephone Counseling and Prayer Services are provided for people who seek spiritual guidance and/or intervention for social problems. On a daily basis, we receive calls from many people with diverse problems, upwards of 80 such calls per month.

The callers have included a woman who lived with a brother who was physically and sexually abusing her and a parent whose son was incarcerated and in need of a residential drug-treatment program. Some of the calls have been from backsliders and ministers who feel they cannot go to their own churches or denominations for spiritual counseling.

Legal Advocacy

The legal aspect of the Care Services provides advocacy for the members of our community. Persons directed to the Care Services are referred either by outside agencies or by word of mouth. Once clients arrive, an assessment of their need is made to determine whether their situation is critical. After a brief interview, each client is advised what procedure will be used in order to protect and enforce their rights. The methods of intervention can include telephone calls, letter writing and/or court appearances. Legal services are provided by appointment only.

Clothing Distribution

Clothing is donated to the Care Services by public and private sources. Distribution is made to the community on Thursdays from 11:30 a.m. until 1:30 p.m. After clients are fed in our Love Kitchen, they are ushered into the parking area and allowed to select the clothing they need. This is done throughout the year.

The Care Services also make possible the distribution of coats, gloves, blankets and toiletry items during the cold winter months.

Over the years, there have been thousands of clothing items donated to our community. This ministry has given us the opportunity to see many people come to Jesus Christ as a result of being clothed.

Conclusion

The Care Services continue to grow and expand their services as the needs of the community arise and as the Lord allows. We firmly believe that one of the avenues which the Lord will continue to use to dispel the deep effects of sin in this area is the services which the Care Services provide. We have witnessed lives being transformed by the power of the Holy Spirit. This brings glory to God, honor to the individual and dignity to the community.